Ilyushin Il-

in action

By Hans-Heiri Stapfer

Color by Don Greer

Illustrated by David Gebhardt and Darren Glenn

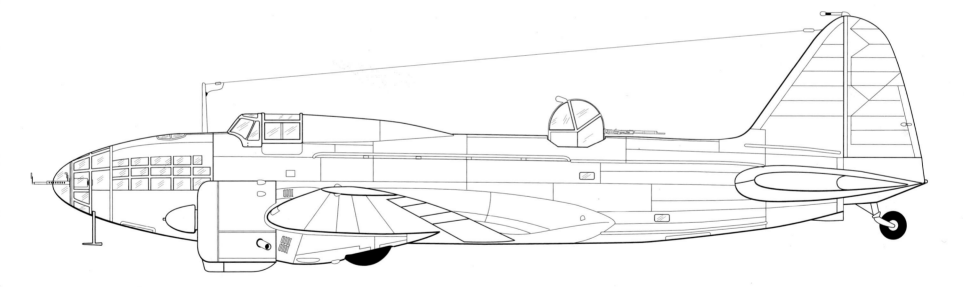

Aircraft Number 192

squadron/signal publications

Searchlights track a pair of Il-4s (White 69 and White 67) attacking German-held positions during World War Two. The Soviets often deployed their Ilyushin DB-3 and Il-4 long-range bombers on night missions, which minimized the risk of German fighter attacks.

Photo Captions and Acknowledgements

Zdenek Hurt

Dusan Mikolas

Zdenek Titz

Carl-Fredrik Geust

Wolfgang Tamme

Hannu Valtonen

Keski-Suomen Ilmailumuseo
   (Finnish Air Force Museum)

Manfred Griehl

Nigel A. Eastaway

Klaus Niska

Russian Aviation Research Trust
   (RART)

Volker Koos

Jakub Marszalkiewicz

Viktor Kulikov

Andrzej Morgala

Harold Thiele

San Diego Aerospace Museum

Ray Wagner

Lennart Andersson

George Punka

Vladimir Gagin

ISBN 0-89747-471-6

If you have any photographs of aircraft, armor, soldiers or ships of any nation, particularly wartime snapshots, why not share them with us and help make Squadron/Signal's books all the more interesting and complete in the future. Any photograph sent to us will be copied and the original returned. The donor will be fully credited for any photos used. Please send them to:

Squadron/Signal Publications, Inc.
1115 Crowley Drive
Carrollton, TX 75011-5010

Если у вас есть фотографии самолётов, вооружения, солдат или кораблей любой страны, особенно, снимки времён войны, поделитесь с нами и помогите сделать новые книги издательства Эскадрон/Сигнал ещё интереснее. Мы переснимем ваши фотографии и вернём оригиналы. Имена приславших снимки будут сопровождать все опубликованные фотографии. Пожалуйста, присылайте фотографии по адресу:

Squadron/Signal Publications, Inc.
1115 Crowley Drive
Carrollton, TX 75011-5010

軍用機、装甲車両、兵士、軍艦などの写真を所持しておられる方はいらっしゃいませんか？どの国のものでも結構です。作戦中に撮影されたものが特に良いのです。Squadron/Signal社の出版する刊行物において、このような写真は内容を一層充実し、興味深くすることができます。当方にお送り頂いた写真は、複写の後お返しいたします。出版物中に写真を使用した場合は、必ず提供者のお名前を明記させて頂きます。お写真は下記にご送付ください。

Squadron/Signal Publications, Inc.
1115 Crowley Drive
Carrollton, TX 75011-5010

A late production Ilyushin Il-4 (White 26) flies towards its target in Eastern Europe. The bomber is camouflaged in overall Black (FS37038), with Dark Green (approximately FS34092) and Medium Green (approx. FS34151) on the upper surfaces. GAM-9 flame damping shrouds are fitted over the exhaust stacks. No national markings are painted on the rear fuselage and wing upper surfaces. Soviet State Aviation Factories built 6784 DB-3s and Il-4s between 1936 and 1946. DB-3s, Il-4s, and North American B-25 Mitchells were the backbone of the Soviet Long-Range Aviation force during the Great Patriotic War of 1941-45. (Viktor Kulikov)

Introduction

The twin-engine **Il-4** long-range bomber was the first design completed by Sergei V. Ilyushin and his *Opytnoe Konstruktorskoe Byuro* (OKB; Experimental Design Bureau). This bomber entered Soviet *Voyenno-Vozdushniye Sily* (VVS; Military Air Forces) service as the **DB-3** in late 1936. DB stood for *Dal'nyi Bombardirovshchik* (Long-Range Bomber). In March of 1942, the designation of the DB-3F variant was changed to Il-4.

This type entered the headlines of the world press when Vladimir K. Kokkinaki and his navigator Mikhail Gordinenko set a world distance record in the **TsKB-30** *Moskva* (Moscow). They departed from Moscow bound for New York on 29 April 1939. Bad weather forced the crew to make an emergency landing at Miskou Island, at the northern tip of New Brunswick, Canada after a flight of 22 hours and 56 minutes. The TsKB-30 *Moskva* had traveled approximately 8000 км (4971 miles) at an average speed of 348 кмн (216 мрн). It became the first Soviet aircraft to land in Canada and on the Eastern Coast of North America.

The DB-3 received its baptism of fire in early 1939, when the Soviets delivered 24 aircraft to China. From its base at Chengdu, the DB-3s flew several raids against the invading Japanese forces. The most successful missions were two raids flown to Hankou, a Japanese held airfield approximately 1500 км (932 miles) from Chengdu.

DB-3s became the first Soviet aircraft to bomb Berlin. A force of 15 DB-3Ts based at a small airstrip at Ösel Island in the Baltic Sea attacked the German capital during the evening of 8 August 1941.

The Il-4 was the sole combat aircraft in the VVS inventory developed in the mid-1930s that was still in front-line service at the end of the Great Patriotic War (the Russian name for the 1941-45 war with Germany.) It served on every front during conflict. Apart from its role as a long-range bomber, the DB-3/Il-4 was successfully deployed on torpedo and long-range reconnaissance missions. Soviet factories built 6784 DB-3s and Il-4s between 1936 and 1946. The Il-4 and US-supplied North American B-25 Mitchells formed the backbone of the *Aviatsiya Dal'niya Destviya* (ADD; Long-Range Aviation) Bomber Regiments during the Great Patriotic War. The Il-4 was the principal Soviet long-range bomber aircraft until the arrival of the Tupolev Tu-4, the Soviet copy of the Boeing B-29 Superfortress. The last Il-4 was withdrawn from operational service in 1952.

The United States of America was a major influence on Ilyushin's bomber. Most DB-3s/Il-4s were manufactured with American-built machinery and tools. Many of the manufacturing techniques and the know-how for the economical mass production of large all-metal aircraft were adopted from the Douglas plant at Santa Monica, California.

TsKB-26 Bomber Prototype

In the early 1930s, the VVS ordered a replacement of the four-engine Tupolev TB-3 long-range bomber. The new bomber was to carry a larger bomb load farther and higher than the existing model. Additionally, the future long-range bomber was to be easily produced in large quantities.

Sergei V. Ilyushin, head of the No. 3 Brigade of the *Tsentral'naya Konstruktorskoe Byuro* (TsKB; Central Design Bureau), began the first research work on a two-engine, long-range bomber as a private venture in early 1933. The project received the designation **TsKB-26**. Apart from the gliders he produced, the TsKB-26 became the first aircraft designed by the 39-year-old Ilyushin.

He envisaged the project with a high aspect ratio wing, which provided less lifting power than the TB-3, but enabled the TsKB-26 to reach higher speeds. Ilyushin's preliminary studies concluded that the new long-range bomber could be developed as a twin-engine cantilever monoplane with lighter, more efficient engines. This design offered a high degree of aerodynamic refinement and airframe weight reduction. The goal was not only attained by reducing the wing area, but also by the advanced airfoil, reducing the fuselage cross-section, internal bomb load carriage, retracting the undercarriage, and stressed smooth skin.

Ilyushin and other young engineers received support from more highly experienced colleagues, including Nikolai Nikolayevich Polikarpov, the Soviet 'Fighter King.' Their influence resulted in the TsKB-26's principal aerodynamic parameters being close to those of high-speed monoplane fighters also under development.

The need for rapid development resulted in the decision to build a simplified prototype to serve as a technology demonstrator. The TsKB-26 combined a wooden fuselage and vertical stabilizer with metal wings and horizontal stabilizers, while production aircraft were designed to be of all-metal construction. A bomb bay was installed, but no bomb racks and defensive armament was fitted. The TsKB-26 was designed to carry a 1000 кг (2205 pound) bomb load.

The lack of a suitable powerplant concerned Ilyushin and his No. 3 Brigade at the project's beginning. The existing 690 нр Mikulin M-34 engine was deemed too heavy and uneconomical. Fortunately, the Soviet Union obtained license production rights to the French Gnome-Rhone 14 Kdrs 'Mistral Major' 14-cylinder two-row radial engine. The task of the license building of the engine was delegated to Sergej K. Tumansky, chief-engineer of the *Tsentral'noe Institut Aviatsionnogo Motorostroeniyua* (TsIAM; Central Institute of Aircraft Engines). The Soviet copy of the Mistral Major received the designation M-85. The first Soviet-built M-85 was delivered from *Gosudarstvennyi Aviatsionnyi Zavod* (GAZ; State

The TsKB-26 prototype was rolled out at Frunze Airfield in Moscow on 1 June 1935. It conducted its maiden flight a few days later. This aircraft had a wooden fuselage, which was replaced by a metal fuselage in the production DB-3. The TsKB-26 captured six world records in 1936 and 1937. (RART)

Aviation Factory) 29 at Zaporozhe in 1934. The M-85, with a take-off output of 765 HP, was chosen to power the TsKB-26 prototype.

TsKB-26 construction began in the TsKB prototype shop at GAZ 39 *Imeni Menzhinskogo*[1] at Moscow-Khodinka in June of 1934. On 29 December 1934, Soviet authorities approved the mock up. The TsKB-26 was rolled out at Khodinka (Frunze) Airfield – Moscow's central airport at the time – on 1 June 1935. A few days later, test pilot Vladimir K. Kokkinaki flew this aircraft on its maiden flight. Kokkinaki had commanded an *Aviatsiya Polk* (AP; Aviation Regiment) before becoming a test pilot for various OKBs in early 1935.

The factory test program showed the TsKB-26 to be stable in flight and normal to handle. Its single engine performance was considered good and its maneuverability far exceeded VVS requirements. The TsKB-26 reached 330 KMH (205 MPH) at sea level and 390 KMH (242 MPH) at 3250 M (10,663 feet). Kokkinaki demonstrated this aircraft's aerobatic qualities during the flight test program. The TsKB-26 became the first Soviet bomber to perform a loop.

After completing the first stage of flight development, the TsKB-26 was demonstrated on 28 August 1935. Witnessing this flight were the Commissar of Defense and chairman of the VVS, Marshal Kliment E. Voroshilov, and Grigory K. Ordzhonikidze, Commissar for Heavy Industry. Both Voroshilov and Ordzhonikidze highly praised the production standards of its wooden details, but noted that the production bomber must be of all-metal construction.

The TsKB-26 participated in the May Day flypast over Moscow on 1 May 1936 – the International Labor Day. This was the first public showing of the new long-range bomber. Soviet *Vozhd* (Leader) Iosif V. Stalin visited GAZ 39 at Khodinka that evening. He met both Ilyushin and test pilot Kokkinaki. Stalin insisted that TsKB-26 flight tests be completed in the shortest possible time, in order to rapidly begin mass production of the new bomber.

In the summer of 1936, the TsKB-26 captured five world records. On 17 July, Kokkinaki flew it to 11,294 M (37,054 feet) with a 500 KG (1102 pound) payload. Nine days later, the TsKB-26 reached 11,402 M (37,408 feet) with a 1000 KG (2205 pound) payload. Kokkinaki improved on both of these records the following month, first by attaining 12,816 M (42,047 feet) with a 500 KG payload on 3 August. He then reached 12,101 M (39,701 feet) with a 1000 KG payload on 21 August. On 7 September 1936, the TsKB-26 lifted a 2000 KG (4409 pound) load to 11,005 M (36,106 feet). Kokkinaki captured a sixth world record on 26 August 1937, when the prototype covered a 5000 KM (3107 mile) closed circuit with a 1000 KG payload at an average speed of 325.4 KMH (202.2 MPH).

TsKB-30 Bomber Prototype

In parallel with the TsKB-26 flight test program, the construction of the upgraded TsKB-30 was under way. This plane served as a pattern for the future production models. It differed from the TsKB-26 by having an all-metal fuselage, a defensive armament of three 7.62MM ShKAS[2] machine guns, and a fully equipped bomb bay. In contrast to the other bombers in VVS service, the TsKB-30 carried its bombs on its central partition, instead of the cassette racks located on the weapon bay sides. Such an arrangement enabled the installation of three additional weapon racks beneath the fuselage. Two of these were carried by the weapon bay beams and the third by the central partition.

Vladimir K. Kokkinaki piloted the TsKB-30 on its maiden flight on 31 March 1936, making this occasion a special birthday gift for chief designer Sergei V. Ilyushin. The factory test pro-

gram proceeded fairly smoothly. The limited longitudinal stability was rectified by the introduction of a horizontal stabilizer (tailplane) with an increased area.

The TsKB-30 prototype was introduced for its two-part State Acceptance Test program in the summer of 1936. The final phase of its acceptance evaluation program was carried both with wheels and ski undercarriage between November of 1936 and May of 1937. State Acceptance tests showed that the TsKB-30's 400 KMH (249 MPH) top speed was only 24 KMH (15 MPH) slower than the Tupolev SB fast medium bomber, but its 4000 KM (2486 mile) range was over twice that of the Tupolev design. The 2900 KG (6393 pound) maximum internal bomb load was nearly five times the SB's 600 KG (1323 pound) internal bomb capacity. Additionally, the TsKB-30's defensive armament had greater firing angles than those of the SB, which resulted in superior defensive effectiveness.

The TsKB-30's tests demonstrated that the increased tailplane area, introduced during the company flight tests, improved longitudinal stability. Test pilots did find fault with the lack of dual controls and aileron trimmers. Another weak point of the TsKB-30 was its complex undercarriage retraction and extension system. Yet another shortcoming detected during the field evaluation was the long refueling time required.

The combat experience of the Tupolev SB-2-M-100-A in Spain during its Civil War also influenced the TsKB-30. The first SBs were delivered to the Soviet-backed Republicans in October of 1936, when TsKB-30 operational testing was under way. Based on the combat experiences in the Spanish civil war, the VVS criticized the lack of self-sealing fuel tanks and an intercom system. Both were considered vital during combat.

Despite its shortcomings, the TsKB-30 was regarded as a highly promising design. Mass production had been ordered in August of 1936, even before the conclusion of the State Acceptance Trials.

Ilyushin's chief test pilot Vladimir K. Kokkinaki stands by the TsKB-26. He flew this aircraft on its maiden flight and during the factory test program. Kokkinaki performed a loop with the TsKB-26 and became the first Soviet pilot to do so with a two-engine bomber. He also flew the aircraft on its world record setting flights. (Viktor Kulikov)

---

[1]*Imeni Menzhinskogo*: Named for Menzhinski. V.P. Menzhinski was chief of the *Obyedinyonnoye Gosudarstvennoye Politicheskoye Upravleniye* (OGPU; United State Political Administration), the Soviet secret police from 1923 to1934.

[2]ShKAS: *Shpital'ny-Komaritski Aviatsionny Skorosteiny*; Shpital'ny-Komaritski Rapid-Firing Aircraft (machine gun).

Development

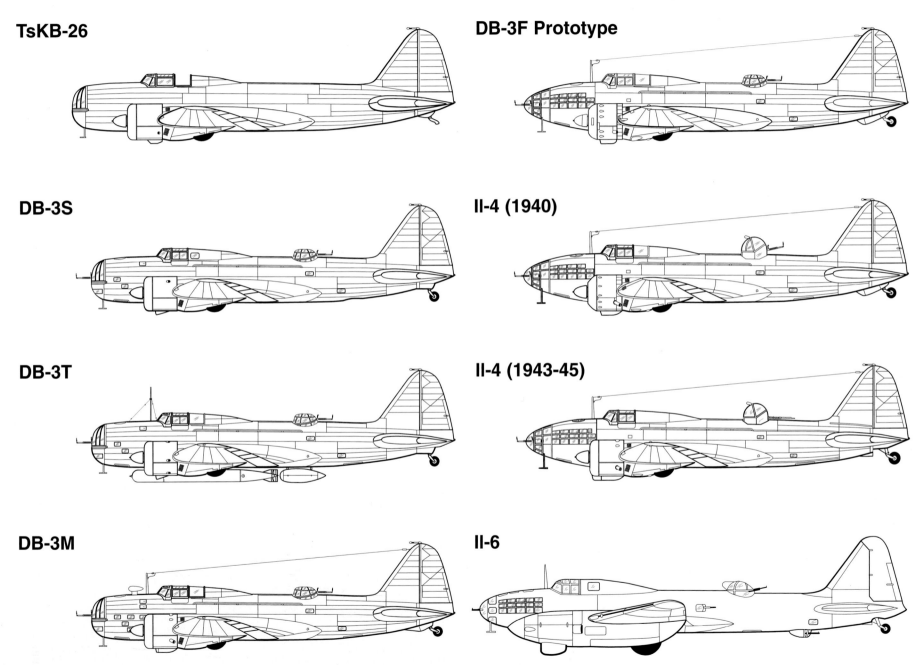

TsKB-26

DB-3F Prototype

DB-3S

Il-4 (1940)

DB-3T

Il-4 (1943-45)

DB-3M

Il-6

Ilyushin DB-3S

GAZ (State Aviation Factory) 39 *Imeni Menzhinskogo* at Moscow-Khodinka began preparing for DB-3 production in August of 1936. The first eight pre-series DB-3s – designated **DB-3S**s – were delivered to the VVS (Soviet Air Force) in late 1936. These bombers were delivered with full bomb carriage and release equipment. They were each armed with one 7.62MM ShKAS machine gun in the TUR-8 nose turret and a further ShKAS in the MV-3 rear upper turret. Provision was made for a third ShKAS to be mounted in the lower fuselage aperture; however, this was not fitted on the DB-3S. The ten wing fuel tanks had a maximum capacity of 2860 L (755.5 gallons).

The DB-3S differed in several details from the TsKB-26 prototype. The former's nose was lengthened by 52 CM (20.5 inches) and three windows were added to each side. Overall length increased from the TsKB-26's 13.7 M (44 feet 11.4 inches) to the DB-3S's 14.22 M (46 feet 7.8 inches). A glazed emergency escape hatch was added atop the nose. The front windshield was modified and an aft sliding cockpit canopy added. (The TsKB-26 prototype had lacked a pilot's canopy.) The cockpit's dorsal fairing was also lengthened. The exhaust stack was relocated from the engine cowling's lower side to the top on the DB-3S. The carburetor air intake was reduced in size on the DB-3S. Two windows were added in the radio-operators compartment in the aft fuselage, and a tail wheel replaced the tail skid.

The DB-3S had a wingspan of 21.44 M (70 feet 4.1 inches) and a height of 4.35 M (14 feet 3.3 inches). It weighed 4778 KG (10,534 pounds) empty and 7000 KG (15,432 pounds) fully loaded. Its two 765 HP M-85 radial engines gave the DB-3S a maximum speed of 400 KMH (249 MPH). The service ceiling was 8400 M (27,559 feet) and its range amounted to 3100 KM (1926 miles). The DB-3S's three man crew consisted of a pilot, navigator/bombardier, and radio operator/rear gunner.

Six of the eight initial production batch DB-3Ss were delivered to the VVS, which was establishing five *Dal'nyi Bombardirovoch'nyi Aviatsion'nyi Polki* (DBAPs; Long-Range Bomber Aviation Regiments). The two remaining aircraft were allocated to the State Aviation Factories as a pattern aircraft for the mass production. This was undertaken at GAZ 39 *Imeni Menzhinskogo* at Moscow-Khodinka and GAZ 18 at Voronezh. The Voronezh-built DB-3s became notorious for their poor workmanship. Their fuel tanks frequently leaked and wheel brakes and undercarriage parts often failed.

Construction of the DB-3 was slowed by the aircraft's structure, which was the most complex of any aircraft built in the Soviet Union through that time. Manufacturing of the wing spars proved troublesome and time consuming. Outer panel spars were made in sections approximately 2 M (6.6 feet) long. These were gas welded and heat treated, then the welding was X-rayed for faults. Inexperienced inspectors were overcautious with interpreting the X-ray images, which resulted in a high rejection rate of the wing spar structures. Their fear of misinterpreting cracks as film blemishes led to the frequent rejection of perfectly serviceable spars. Another source of production troubles was the use of extra hard 30KhMA crome-molybden steel. This material was used on most of the high-stress airframe parts. The Ilyushin OKB took all possible measures to overcome these problems and improve production rates, including formation of special technical support brigades for addressing these issues. GAZ 39 completed only 33 DB-3s during 1937, while GAZ 18 finished a meager 12 aircraft.

The M-85 radial engines built at GAZ 29 in Zaporozhe were another source of concern. Many Soviet-built parts were of poor quality, resulting in key engine components being imported from aboard. These parts included Voltex ROD 14 BA magnetos, Stromberg NAR 125 G carburetors, and BG3RK spark plugs.

The 1937 batch DB-3S was 280 KG (617 pounds) heavier than the DB-3S pre-series aircraft built in 1936, due to internal equipment changes. During this period, the VVS prepared concrete runways at least 1000 M (3281 feet) long at airbases scheduled to host DB-3s. This standard was based on the minimum take off run of a fully laden DB-3.

The first eight pre-production DB-3S bombers were delivered to the VVS (Soviet Air Force) in late 1936. Only three windows per side were fitted to the navigator's compartment on this initial variant. The Soviets imported magnetos, carburetors, and spark plugs to properly run the M-85 radial engines. (Viktor Kulikov)

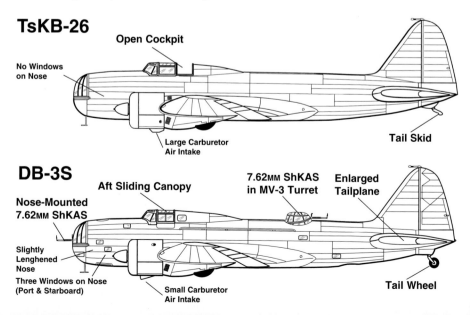

TsKB-26

No Windows on Nose

Open Cockpit

Large Carburetor Air Intake

Tail Skid

DB-3S

Aft Sliding Canopy

7.62MM ShKAS in MV-3 Turret

Enlarged Tailplane

Nose-Mounted 7.62MM ShKAS

Slightly Lengthened Nose

Three Windows on Nose (Port & Starboard)

Small Carburetor Air Intake

Tail Wheel

Ilyushin DB-3B

The M-86 14-cylinder, air-cooled, radial engine – an improved version of the M-85 – became available in early 1938. The new engine's 950 HP take off rating was 185 HP greater than the M-85's 765 HP take off rating. The M-86's weight of 609 KG (1343 pounds) was only 9 KG (20 pounds) greater than the M-85's 600 KG (1323 pound) weight. The M-85 ran on 87 octane aviation gasoline, while the M-86 used 90 to 92 octane fuel for greater performance.

Two M-86 engines powered the **DB-3B**. These engines originally turned V-85 three-bladed fixed pitch metal propellers, which had a diameter of 3.4 M (11 feet 1.9 inches). The V-85 was replaced on later DB-3Bs by the VISh-3[1] three-bladed metal propeller, which had two pitch settings. This propeller had a slightly larger spinner fitted over the hub and a diameter of 3.25 M (10 feet 8 inches).

The DB-3B had five windows per side on its navigator-navigator compartment, compared to three per side on the earlier DB-3S. The additional windows improved the navigator-bombardier's view out the aircraft's side.

Three different type of bomb racks (DER-19, DER-21 and DER-31) were fitted inside the bomb bay, depending on the bombs carried. Bombs ranged in size from 8 KG (17.6 pounds) to 1000 KG (2205 pounds). These weapons were released by the ESBR-2 releasing mechanism located in the navigator-bombardier's compartment. The bombing results were recorded with an AFA-B camera, which operated in three settings: vertical, 15° aft, or 45° aft. Both the DB-3S and DB-3B were equipped with the new OPB-2 optical bomb sight. The Boykow factory built this device, which was based on the German Goerz bombsight.

The DB-3B was also operated as a long-range reconnaissance aircraft, using an AFA-33 cam-

[1]VISh: *Vint c Izmenyaemovo Shaga*; Variable-Pitch Propeller.

An overall natural metal DB-3B undergoes an engine check in the winter of 1938. The DB-3B was equipped with the M-86 engine, which was an improvement of the earlier M-85. This variant had five windows per side on the navigator's compartment, compared to three per side on the previous DB-3S. DB-3Bs were fully equipped with bomb sights and racks and defensive machine guns. (RART)

era mounted in the bomb bay and remotely operated by the navigator-bombardier. Heating equipment on the AFA-33 assured its proper operation in the extreme cold of high altitude winter operations.

The defense armament consisted of three 7.62MM ShKAS machine guns in single mounts. One weapon was mounted in the nose TUR-8 turret with 500 rounds of ammunition. The angle of fire was 50° to both sides and -60° to +90° elevation The MV-3 turret on the upper rear fuselage provided a 360° field of fire. This ShKAS was supplied with 1000 rounds. The lower rear gun position with 500 rounds had a limited angle of fire of 25° to both port and starboard sides.

Flight navigation instruments included an AG-1 artificial horizon and a GMK-2 gyroscopic compass. The long-range communication was provided using an RSB *Dvina* radio, while communication between aircraft in formation was performed with an RSVS-1 *Luch* Very High Frequency (VHF) transceiver. Communication between the navigator-bombardier, pilot, and radio operator in the rear fuselage was accomplished using the SPU-3 intercom system. Provision was made for the RPK-2 radio compass and target finding device, which was placed ahead of the cockpit. The RPK-2 – based on the American Bendix device – was not fitted on all DB-3s. The AGP-1 two-channel autopilot was fitted in several DB-3s.

DB-3Bs were delivered in a natural metal overall finish, with national markings painted on the aft fuselage and upper and lower port and starboard wing surfaces. This insignia consisted of a red five-pointed star thinly outlined in black.

In early 1938, a third DB-3 production line was established at GAZ 126 in Komsomolsk-na-Amur. This factory completed 30 DB-3s by the end of 1938. GAZ 126 was equipped with the most modern production machinery and systems, with most equipment of American origin. The US delivered 20,000 machine tools worth 70 million US Dollars to the Soviet State Aviation Factories prior to World War Two.

Nose Section Development

DB-3S

Three Windows on Side
(Port & Starboard)

DB-3B

Antenna Mast
(Optional)

Five Windows on Side
(Port & Starboard)

Ilyushin DB-3T

In 1937, the Ilyushin OKB cooperated with the Scientific and Research Mine and Torpedo Establishment of the *Voenno-Morskoi Flot* (VMF; Soviet Navy) at Leningrad (now St. Petersburg), with the aim of developing a torpedo carrier based on the DB-3B.

Two 765 HP M-85 engines turning V-85 propellers powered the **DB-3T** (*torpedonosyets*; torpedo carrier) prototype, which first flew in 1938. The 800 HP M-86 replaced the M-85 on production DB-3Ts. A number of these torpedo carriers were retrofitted with the M-87 engine and the VISh-3 propeller. Several DB-3Ts were later retrofitted with M-87 engines turning VISh-3 propellers. The DB-3T's airframe was approximately 480 KG (1058 pounds) lighter than that of the DB-3B bomber, due to removal of level bombing equipment.

One torpedo was mounted on a T-18 pylon located on the DB-3T's centerline. The VMF used the 45-CM (17.7-inch) Type 45-36-AN (*aviatsionno-nizkoye*; low airdrop) torpedo for low-altitude release and the Type 45-36-AM torpedo for shallow waters. These low level launched torpedoes were released at an altitude of 30 M (98 feet) at approximately 240 KMH (149 MPH) using a nose-mounted PTN-4 or PTN-5 sight. The Type 45-36-AV (*aviatsionno-vysokoye*; high airdrop) torpedo was dropped from an altitude between 250 M (820 feet) and 400 M (1312 feet). An OPB-1M sight mounted in the aircraft's nose guided the weapon's launch. The Type 45-36-AV torpedo was provided with a parachute to slow its fall to the water. Once the parachute dropped off when the torpedo entered the water, the weapon traveled in a spiral path towards the target. All Type 45-36 torpedo variants weighed 940 KG (2072 pounds) and had a 200 KG (441 pounds) high explosive warhead. The Type 45-36 was a copy of the Italian *Fiume* (River) torpedoes. Soviet torpedoes based on the *Fiume* type were far from reliable at first, primarily due to problems with the delay fuse mechanism.

The DB-3T was a lighter aircraft than the DB-3B; however, increased drag from the externally mounted torpedo reduced the DB-3T's maximum speed and range compared to the DB-3B bomber. Early DB-3Ts had an antenna mast in front of the cockpit supported by four bracing wires. Late production aircraft had a conical antenna mast without bracing wires.

The DB-3T was also operated as a mine-layer on occasion. One 900 KG (1984 pound) AMG-1 sea mine measuring 3.5 M (11.5 feet) in length was carried under the fuselage. Alternatively, a 1000 KG (2205 pound) *Geyro* anchored mine was carried. The DB-3T also carried two 500 KG (1102 pound) MDM-500 seabed mines using special racks fitted to the lower fuselage.

The DB-3T successfully completed the State Acceptance Trials and a first batch of torpedo-bombers was built in mid-1938. They were delivered in an overall light gray camouflage with national markings painted on the upper and lower wing surfaces and the rear fuselage. The Soviet red star had a small black outline.

DB-3T crews, trained for torpedo and mine attacks at sea, quickly switched to conventional bombing missions after German forces invaded the Soviet Union on 22 June 1941. Two days after the Germans launched their assault (Operation BARBAROSSA), DB-3Ts of the 1st *Mino-Torpednaya Aviatsiya Polk* (MTAP; Mine-Torpedo Aviation Regiment), VVS of the *Krasnoznamyonny Baltiiski Flot* (KBF; Red Banner Baltic Fleet[1]) bombed the German-held port of Memel (now Laipeda, Latvia).

DB-3Ts of the 1st MTAP were also the first Soviet aircraft to attack the German capital of Berlin. On the evening of 7 August 1941, 15 DB-3Ts took off from Kagul aerodrome at Ösel Island in the Baltic Sea off Estonia and headed via Stolpmünde for Berlin, 1760 KM (1094 miles) away. Each aircraft dropped eight 100 KG (220 pound) FAB-100[2] bombs on the city's outskirts, which caused little damage. This raid took the Germans by total surprise and no

An overall light gray DB-3T (Red 1) is armed with a 45 CM (17.7 inch) Type 45-36-AN torpedo. National markings are painted on the upper and lower wing surfaces and the rear fuselage. Shortly after the outbreak of the Great Patriotic War on 22 June 1941, DB-3Ts were camouflaged with Light Green and Dark Green upper surfaces. (RART)

DB-3Ts were lost to enemy action. The attack was repeated the next day, but one DB-3T was shot down over Berlin. The bombs released hit uninhabited territory north of the city. Ten raids were flown against Berlin during August and September of 1941.

Shortly after the outbreak of the Great Patriotic War, most DB-3Ts were camouflaged with Light Green and Dark Green upper surfaces. For more than a year, the DB-3Ts were primarily engaged in conventional bombing missions. This situation changed in the summer of 1942, when they increased their attacks on German vessels. The DB-3T served through the entire conflict and several also saw action against Japan in August of 1945.

A natural metal Type 45-36-AN torpedo is fitted on a T-18 rack mounted on the DB-3T's centerline. This Soviet torpedo was copied from the Italian *Fiume* torpedo. This DB-3T was delivered with M-86 engines, but was later retrofitted with M-87s and the VISh-3 variable pitch propellers. The small carburetor air intake under the engine cowling is typical for DB-3Ts originally powered by the M-86. This variant had a slim antenna mast, instead of the thicker, conical antenna that equipped late production DB-3 bombers. (RART)

---

[1] Red Banner Baltic Fleet. The Baltic Fleet was bestowed the Order of the Red Banner for its service in the October Revolution in 1917. It received a second Order of the Red Banner for its Great Patriotic War efforts.

[2] FAB: *Fugasnaya Aviatsionnaya Bomba*; General Purpose Aviation Bomb.

The VMF (Soviet Navy) evaluated the DB-3TP floatplane at Sevastopol on the Black Sea between 22 June and 28 September 1938. The DB-3TP rests on a ground handling dolly and carries a Type 45-36-AN torpedo. The floatplane was equipped with M-86 engines turning V-85 propellers. Additional entry handhold rails were mounted in front of the cockpit canopy and between the dorsal cockpit fairing and the MV-3 turret. (Viktor Kulikov)

The port M-86 engine was removed from the DB-3TP and placed on a nearby raft. This raft supports three sailors who serviced this powerplant. The sole DB-3TP became the last combat floatplane built in the Soviet Union. (RART)

Ilyushin DB-3TP

The VVS VMF (Soviet Naval Aviation) lacked sufficient shore based airfields in the White and Barents seas and Pacific Ocean coast areas. This restricted the DB-3T's deployment in these regions. In 1938, the VMF ordered a floatplane version of the DB-3T to meet this requirement.

A standard production DB-3S was converted into the **DB-3TP** (*torpedonosyets poplavkovyi*; torpedo carrier floatplane). Two Type Zh floats purchased from Britain's Short Brothers Ltd. replaced the conventional landing gear. The landing gear was deleted and the main wheel wells were faired over. Hand rails were mounted on both sides of the nose in front of the cockpit and on each fuselage side between the dorsal cockpit fairing's end and the MV-3 gun turret. Two M-86 engines turning V-85 propellers powered the DB-3TP.

The T-18 pylon mounted on the centerline held either one 45 см (17.7 inch) Type 45-36 torpedo or one 900 кг (1984 pound) AMG-1 sea mine. Two additional pylons flanked the T-18 to carry 400 кг (882 pounds) of bombs. No defensive armament was fitted during the aircraft's factory test and field evaluation trials.

The DB-3TP prototype was built in early 1938 and test pilot Vladimir K. Kokkinaki flew the factory test trials at Rybinsk dam. The type had been recommended for series production and the VVS VMF ordered 15 DB-3TPs even before field evaluation began.

The VVS VMF held the field evaluation trials at Sevastopol on the Black Sea between 22 June and 28 September 1938. These tests exposed the DB-3TP's shortcomings, which included difficult maintenance and armament loading. The aircraft required a specialized infrastructure, including hangars, slips, and fuel and armament depots. Its performance was considerably inferior to the DB-3S. A torpedo-laden DB-3TP reached a top speed of 373 кмн (232 мрн), which was 27 кмн (17 мрн) slower than the wheel-equipped DB-3.

The trials results prompted the VMF to cancel its order for 15 DB-3TPs and increase the number of shore based airfields in the regions of the Northern and Pacific fleets. The single DB-3TP was the last Soviet combat floatplane built.

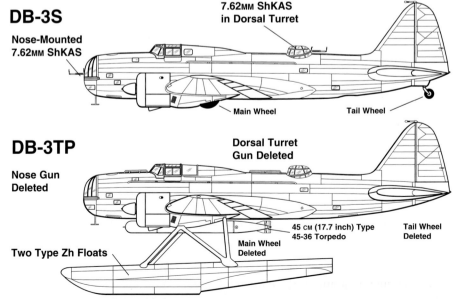

DB-3S

Nose-Mounted 7.62mm ShKAS

7.62mm ShKAS in Dorsal Turret

Main Wheel

Tail Wheel

DB-3TP

Nose Gun Deleted

Dorsal Turret Gun Deleted

45 см (17.7 inch) Type 45-36 Torpedo

Main Wheel Deleted

Tail Wheel Deleted

Two Type Zh Floats

DB-3T (Experimental)

The VMF (Soviet Navy) requested a torpedo carrying aircraft with a closed, heated torpedo bay in June of 1938. The Ilyushin OKB responded to this request by converting a standard DB-3T.

This experimental DB-3T was equipped with a three-piece torpedo covering made of aluminum alloy along the lower fuselage. Prior to torpedo release, the two main doors opened outward and the nose covering opened to starboard.

Hot exhaust gases collected from the exhaust stacks supplied heated air for the torpedo bay. These gases were fed from a tube connected from each exhaust stack to the bay. The entire torpedo covering had a number of hatches that could be opened. These hatches allowed excess exhaust gas to escape from the torpedo bay.

The DB-3T (experimental) was based on a DB-3B airframe; however, M-87A engines replaced the original M-86 engines during the aircraft's service life. Small carburetor intakes were typical for DB-3s powered by M-85 and M-86 engines.

This DB-3T (experimental) was not fitted with armament or weapons equipment. The national markings – red stars with thin black outlines – were painted on the upper and lower port and starboard wing surfaces and the aft fuselage sides of the natural metal airframe.

The VMF conducted trials with the experimental DB-3T over the Baltic Sea during 1938. These trials showed that the DB-3T could not carry the larger diameter AMG-1 and *Geyro* type sea mines within the closed torpedo bay. The bay restricted the aircraft's armament to torpedoes. This resulted in cancellation of the converted DB-3T trials and this process was ended.

This DB-3T was modified with a covered and heated torpedo bay. The airframe was originally based on the DB-3B, but was later powered by M-87 engines. This particular aircraft retains the small carburetor intakes adopted from the M-86-powered DB-3s. Thin black outlines are painted on the red national markings. (RART)

A tube connected to each exhaust stack fed heated air for the torpedo bay. The tube led from the exhaust stack into the fuselage. Four open hatches are located along the torpedo bay fairing. (RART)

The port and starboard torpedo bay doors are opened on this experimental DB-3T. This action was performed to load, service, and drop the Type 45-36 torpedo. The front covering opened to starboard immediately prior to torpedo release. (RART)

Capsule DB-3

An assault transport version of the DB-3 began flight testing in July of 1938. The centerline fuselage racks were modified to carry a D-20 cabin designed by Engineer A. Privalov. Ten fully equipped soldiers were accommodated in the aerodynamically clean capsule. A side opening door on the container's rear allowed paratroopers to exit the DB-3 in flight. Three small windows were cut in the cabin ahead of this capsule.

The DB-3's crew could jettison the capsule in an emergency situation. Attachment of the D-20 capsule required only minor modifications to the lower fuselage. The DB-3 with the D-20 was primarily intended to drop paratroops over enemy positions; however, this container could also be used behind enemy lines on commando operations.

The overall natural metal DB-3 used on the D-20 cabin tests received a new layout for the side window configuration on the nose and no armament was carried. An RPK-2 radio compass was installed atop the nose.

Further experiments were carried out with the DB-3 serving as a drop aircraft for various weapons and equipment. For this reason, a platform able to accommodate up to 1000 KG (2205 pounds) of freight was mounted. This DB-3 successfully dropped motorcycles, 45MM cannon, and a 120MM mortar by parachute during these trials.

Despite successful trials, the *Raboche-Kres'yanskii Krasnyi Armiya* (RKKA; Workers' and Peasants' Red Army) did not adopt this configuration and the troop carrier DB-3 was cancelled.

This DB-3 was equipped with a D-20 cabin for ten fully equipped soldiers on the lower fuselage. DB-3 assault transport trials began in July of 1938. These trials were unsuccessful and the configuration never entered VVS service. The DB-3 has a non-standard navigator's compartment window configuration. Most DB-3s had three to five windows per side on the nose. (Viktor Kulikov)

Two struts supported the nose-mounted data boom of this experimental DB-3B, which was assigned for testing at a Soviet aviation testing establishment. The M-87A-powered DB-3B is camouflaged with Light Green and Dark Green upper surfaces and Light Blue undersurfaces. (Viktor Kulikov)

DB-3 Experimental

A number of experimental DB-3s were built and used for various tests. A DB-3B received a data-boom on the upper nose attached with two suspension booms on the nose. This boom allowed the aircraft to collect data free of interference from airflow immediately in front of the airframe. No armament was carried on this aircraft.

This experimental DB-3 was built on the DB-3B airframe, but the aircraft had received the M-87 engines with three additional apertures in the engine cowling. Additionally, the carburetor intake on the engine cowling's lower side was enlarged.

The aircraft was camouflaged in a light green and dark green upper surface scheme, with a red star painted on the aft fuselage.

The *Tsentral'nyi Aerogirodinamicheskii Institut* (TsAGI; Central Aero and Hydrodynamic Institute) at Moscow extensively employed other DB-3s in testing roles. Several trials were carried out with various shapes and airfoils carried aloft on DB-3s.

TsKB-30 *Moskva*

Record breaking flights proved an effective method to announce new aircraft and to determine their capabilities under various conditions. These flights also proved excellent propaganda for the manufacturing country. In the 1930s, the Soviet Union sought diplomatic relations with several countries. Non-aggression pacts were signed with both China and Estonia in 1932. In November of 1933, the USSR had established diplomatic relations with the United States.

The Soviet supreme command assumed that a nonstop flight from Moscow to New York would garner headlines in the world press. Such a flight would show the world that the Soviet Union had the capability to build aircraft for long distance flights. The record flight was of a friendly nature, but it signaled Western Europe – especially Nazi Germany – that such an aircraft could also carry bombs over long distances. A transatlantic flight via Scandinavia to Canada would have its risks. Stormy weather conditions and strong headwinds over the route would challenge the capabilities of both aircraft and crew.

In early 1938, authorization was given to build a distance record aircraft based on the DB-3B bomber. The technical documentation for the record breaking aircraft – named the TsKB-30 *Moskva* (Moscow) – was issued to the production facilities on 8 April 1938. G.M. Litvinovich's engine team fully revised the M-86 engine's fuel and oil systems.

All armament and combat systems – including bomb racks, bomb sights, and bomb release equipment – was removed from the TsKB-30 *Moskva*. The lower fuselage gun position was faired over and both the MV-3 upper turret and the fuselage aperture were deleted. Additional fuel tanks in the bomb bay and the rear fuselage were installed. These enabled the TsKB-30 *Moskva* to reach an estimated range of 8000 KM (4971 miles), twice that of a standard production DB-3B. The TsKB-30 *Moskva* received the latest flight control, navigation, and radio equipment available in the Soviet Union. Additionally, an oxygen system for the long flight at high altitude was installed. This system was not fitted to standard production DB-3Bs. The fully loaded TsKB-30 *Moskva* had a take off weight of 12,600 KG (27,778 pounds), which was 5600 KG (12,346 pounds) more than on a DB-3S.

Whereas the DB-3B had two small side windows behind the aft sliding cockpit canopy, the TsKB-30 featured a raised cockpit canopy and a large rear window aft of the canopy frame. The *Moskva* also had an enlarged dorsal fairing and six windows fitted to each side of the nose. The latter allowed the navigator an improved view than in the bomber version. Two addition-

al venturi tubes were mounted in front of the portside starboard windows. The TsKB-30 *Moskva* had two pitot heads placed on each side under the nose, instead of the DB-3B's one pitot head under the port nose. The antenna mast was mounted ahead of the TsKB-30's windshield.

The TsKB-30 *Moskva* rolled out on 15 May 1938 and Vladimir K. Kokkinaki piloted it on its maiden flight the next day. Kokkinaki and Navigator A. M. Bryandinsky made the aircraft's first long distance flight on 22 June 1938. The *Moskva* took off from Chkalovskaya aerodrome in Moscow and flew to Spassk-Dalny, approximately 200 KM (124 miles) north of Vladivostok in the Far Eastern Soviet Union. The TsKB-30's 24 hour 38 minute flight covered 7580 KM (4710 miles) at an average speed of 307 KMH (191 MPH). Kokkinaki and Bryandinsky were each named a Hero of the Soviet Union for this flight on 17 July 1938.

The TsKB-30 *Moskva* was then flown to GAZ 39 at Khodinka for refurbishing. It received additional equipment for its Transatlantic flight, including an inflatable rubberized fabric bag for emergency flotation in the forward fuselage. Additionally, the TsKB-30 received the new 950 HP (take off rating) M-87A powerplant. This engine had a BSM-14 ignition system and an AK-87 carburetor. The M-87-powered TsKB-30 *Moskva* had an enlarged carburetor intake and three additional small exhaust stacks compared to the DB-3B.

The flight to New York was scheduled for the fall of 1938, but Bryandinsky was killed in the crash of a Tupolev TB-3 bomber that September. No trained navigator was immediately available and the North Atlantic weather was worsening, which prompted postponement of the record flight until the following spring.

On the afternoon of 29 April 1939, Kokkinaki and new navigator Mikhail Gordinenko took off from Moscow in an attempt to fly nonstop via the great circle route to New York. The first objective was Iceland, but the TsKB-30 encountered strong headwinds as it crossed the Norwegian coastline at 5500 M (18,045 feet). The autopilot failed at this point, requiring Kokkinaki to take manual control for the remainder of the flight. The 'Moskva' was considerably behind schedule by the time it overflew Reykjavik, Iceland. Cape Farewell, at extreme southern Greenland, was crossed at 7000 M (22,966 feet). Fortunately for the crew, the winds suddenly reversed direction and the aircraft's ground speed suddenly increased from 280 KMH

The TsKB-30 *Moskva* (Moscow) was a DB-3 variant employed for long-range record breaking flights. Vladimir K. Kokkinaki and navigator Mikhail Gordinenko took off from Moscow on the afternoon of 29 April 1939. They departed on an attempt to fly nonstop to New York. The overall red TsKB-30 has MOSKVA in white Cyrillic letters on the wing undersurfaces. (RART)

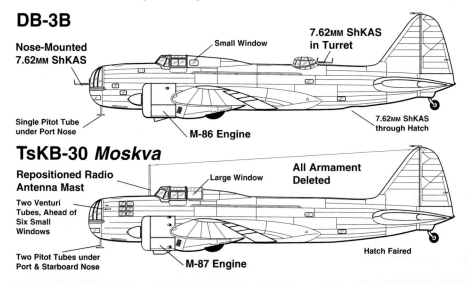

DB-3B

- Nose-Mounted 7.62MM ShKAS
- Small Window
- 7.62MM ShKAS in Turret
- Single Pitot Tube under Port Nose
- M-86 Engine
- 7.62MM ShKAS through Hatch

TsKB-30 *Moskva*

- Repositioned Radio Antenna Mast
- Large Window
- All Armament Deleted
- Two Venturi Tubes, Ahead of Six Small Windows
- Two Pitot Tubes under Port & Starboard Nose
- M-87 Engine
- Hatch Faired

(174 мрн) to 499 кмн (310 мрн). Extremely bad weather forced the aircraft up to an altitude of 9000 м (29,528 feet),where the temperature was -54° Celsius (-65° Fahrenheit). It was learned over the radio that the US coastline was closed in for hundreds of miles. The oxygen supply was by now virtually exhausted and Kokkinaki had no recourse but to descend through thick cloud over the Gulf of St. Lawrence. Dropping almost to ground level, where visibility proved to be scarcely 250 м (820 feet), the Soviet crew fortuitously saw the beam of a lighthouse and attempted an emergency landing in the vicinity. The TsKB-30 *Moskva* made a wheels-up landing on marshland on the small island of Miskou, at the northern tip of New Brunswick, Canada.

The *Moskva* – the first Soviet aircraft to land on North America's East Coast – set a new world distance record. The TsKB-30 flew almost 8000 км (4971 miles) in 22 hours and 56 minutes, with an average speed of 348 кмн (216 мрн).

TsKB-30 N-1 *Ukraina*

The VKP(b)[1] authorized long distance record flights with female crews for propaganda purposes at the end of 1938. It took 18 months to select a suitable aircraft, which was a modified DB-3. Two specially converted aircraft were built at GAZ 39 at Moscow-Khodinka, designated **TsKB-30 N-1** and **TsKB-30 N-2**. Modified M-87 engines turning VISh-3T propellers powered these aircraft. The navigator compartment's window layout was changed from that of the TsKB-30 *Moskva*. Two additional windows were installed and both venturi tubes on the port nose side were slightly relocated.

The TsKB-30 N-1 flew the route between Khabarovsk and Lvov (now Lviv, Ukraine), while the TsKB-30 N-2 flew on the Moscow–Sverdlovsk (now Ekaterinburg)–Sevastopol–Moscow route, a distance of over 5000 км (3107 miles). On 5 July 1940, pilots Maria Mikhalyeva and Nina Rusakova and navigator Maria Nesterenko took off aboard the TsKB-30 N-2. Due to deteriorating weather, the crew was ordered by radio to land and the aircraft touched down near Sverdlovsk, east of the Ural Mountains.

On 27 July 1940, this same crew took off from Khabarovsk near the Chinese frontier in the Far Eastern Soviet Union for its Trans Soviet-Union flight. They were bound for the Ukrainian Soviet Socialist Republic, which became a part of the Soviet Union in December of 1920. The choice of the Khabarovsk–Lvov route was not accidental. On 17 September 1939, the RKKA (Red Army) invaded Eastern Poland and absorbed the former Polish territory into the Ukrainian Socialist Soviet Republic.[2] This also included Lvov (formerly Lemberg), which was the capital of the Austro-Hungarian province of Galicia. The VKP(b) demonstrated through this flight that the former Polish territory was now an integral part of the Soviet Union.

The TsKB-30 N-1 was named *Ukraina* (Ukraine), with the name painted on both sides of the nose. A storm was encountered during the flight and one engine failed after crossing the 1894 м (6214 feet) high Ural Mountain range. The *Ukraina* virtually descended to ground level when the crew managed to restart the engine. Aware of these difficulties, the flight center ordered the three women to proceed with a forced landing. Mikhalyeva and Rusakova made a powerless belly landing in a meadow in the Kirov region, approximately 2200 км (1367 miles) from Lvov. Both VISh-3T propellers were slightly bent on the forced landing. The 'Ukraina' had traveled nearly 7000 км (4350 miles) in 23 hours and 32 minutes, which set a new world distance record for female crews. Since the 'Ukraina' never reached Lvov, the VKP(b) did not broadcast this flight.

[1]VKP(b): *Vsesoyuznaya Kommunisticheskaya Partiya (bol'shevikov)*; All-Union Community Party (Bolshevik). This organization was renamed the Communist Party of the Soviet Union in 1952.

[2]The Soviet Union was secretly allocated this territory by the Nazi-Soviet Pact signed on 23 August 1939. German Foreign Minister Joachim von Ribbentrop and Soviet Foreign Minister Vyacheslav Molotov concluded this agreement.

The TsKB-30 *Moskva* landed wheels up in marshland on Miskou Island at the northern tip of New Brunswick, Canada. It flew almost 8000 км (4971 miles) from Moscow in 22 hours and 56 minutes. This flight to North America secured a long distance record for the Soviet Union. (RART)

The TsKB-30 N-1 *Ukraina* (Ukraine) is lifted on its undercarriage after a belly landing in the Kirov region on 28 July 1940. Both VISh-3T propellers were slightly bent and the two pitot heads were damaged in this landing. An all-female crew flew the 'Ukraina' almost 7000 км (4350 miles) in 23 hours and 32 minutes. (Viktor Kulikov)

Ilyushin DB-3M

Three State Aircraft Factories began producing the **DB-3M** (*modernizirovanyi*; modernized) in the spring of 1938. This variant was a DB-3 powered by the new M-87A radial engine. Suffixes denoting each individual variant were seldom used at the Division and Regiment levels and the aircraft was simply called the DB-3.

The Tumansky M-87A 14-cylinder, air-cooled, radial engine was derived from the M-86. The compression ratio was increased from 5.5 to 6.1 through reducing the cylinder head bottom's curvature. The pistons were fitted with an additional ring. The M-87A's diameter of 129.3 CM (50.9 inches) was 1.3 CM (0.5 inch) less than the M-86. The M-87 was rated at 855 HP in cruise, which was a 135 HP increase over the M-86. The engines were each rated at 950 HP on take off. Weight increased from 609 KG (1343 pounds) on the M-86 to 617 KG (1360 pounds) on the M-87A. Soviet parts replaced all foreign items on the M-87A, including substituting BSM-14 magnetos for Voltex ROD 14 BAs and K-87 carburetors for Stromberg NAR 125s.

The DB-3M had a modified exhaust stack system, which had an additional long exhaust on the lower engine cowling's port side. Two small exhaust stacks were mounted on the starboard side. A circular oil cooler intake was located on the inboard wing leading edge near the engine cowling. Early DB-3s lacked these intakes.

Development of the TsKB-30 *Moskva* in early 1938 influenced the DB-3M's design. The cockpit section was raised and was equipped with a larger dorsal fairing. The two small side windows behind the canopy frame were replaced by a large transparent section. The raised canopy provided the pilot with a far better field of view. Safe taxiing on earlier DB-3s was only possible by having the navigator stand in the open astrodome and guiding the pilot using hand signals.

Several nose window layouts were used during the DB-3M production cycle. Early production aircraft had the DB-3B's five nose window configuration, but subsequent production batches had seven side windows in the navigator-bombardier compartment.

The all-metal DB-3M had a wingspan of 21.44 M (70 feet 4.1 inches), a length of 14.22 M (46 feet 7.8 inches), and a height of 4.35 M (14 feet 3.3 inches). It weighed 5030 KG (11,089 pounds) empty and 7442 KG (16,407 pounds) fully loaded. The DB-3M had a maximum speed of 345 KMH (214 MPH), a service ceiling of 9600 M (31,496 feet), and a maximum range of 3821 KM (2374 miles). It had a crew of three: pilot, navigator-bombardier, and radio operator-rear gunner.

The aircraft was armed with three 7.62MM ShKAS machine guns in single mounts. One weapon with 1100 rounds was mounted in the TUR-8 nose turret, a second gun with 1100 rounds was mounted in the fully rotating MV-3 dorsal turret, and a third gun with 600 rounds fired through the ventral hatch. The DB-3M had a maximum bomb load of 2900 KG (6393 pounds), with 1000 KG (2205 pounds) carried inside the bomb bay.

Several DB-3Ms were equipped with a single DER-19 bomb rack on the wing undersurfaces. Each DER-19 held a bomb load of 250 KG (551 pounds). The external bomb load could only be carried on short-range missions, where less fuel compensated the additional bomb weight.

Early DB-3M operations demonstrated reliability problems with the M-87A engine. The M-87B became available in the fall of 1938. This engine had a strengthened crankcase and wear resistant cylinders with nitric treated surfaces. The M-87B was equipped with the improved AK-87 carburetor, which replaced the older K-87. It turned a VISh-3 three-bladed metal propeller, which had R-2 revolution governors that allowed a pitch range of 22°. Without the R-2, the VISh-3 could be only operated in two settings. The M-87A powered DB-3Ms had a small, triangle shaped carburetor air intake adopted from the DB-3B, but the M-87B equipped bomber received a larger, rectangular shaped carburetor air intake.

Several changes occurred during DB-3M production, including fitting a single venturi tube on the starboard nose side below the cockpit of several aircraft. Some DB-3Ms had this tube located on the port side. Several DB-3Ms were equipped with a radio mast in front of the cockpit. The RPK-2 radio compass was placed on several aircraft in front of the radio mast atop the

A natural metal DB-3M (Blue 2) flies over the Soviet Union in the late 1930s. This early production aircraft has M-87A engines and small, triangular carburetor intakes. This particular DB-3M has both an antenna mast and an RPK-2 Radio Direction Finder (RDF), the latter in the teardrop-shaped fairing on the nose. Both items were not fitted to all DB-3s. The venturi tube under the cockpit was rarely fitted on the port side. (Viktor Kulikov)

DB-3B

M-86 Engine

Aperture for 7.62MM ShKAS

DB-3M

RPK-2 RDF Antenna

M-87B Engine

Movable Windows for 7.62MM ShKAS on LUMV-2 Mount

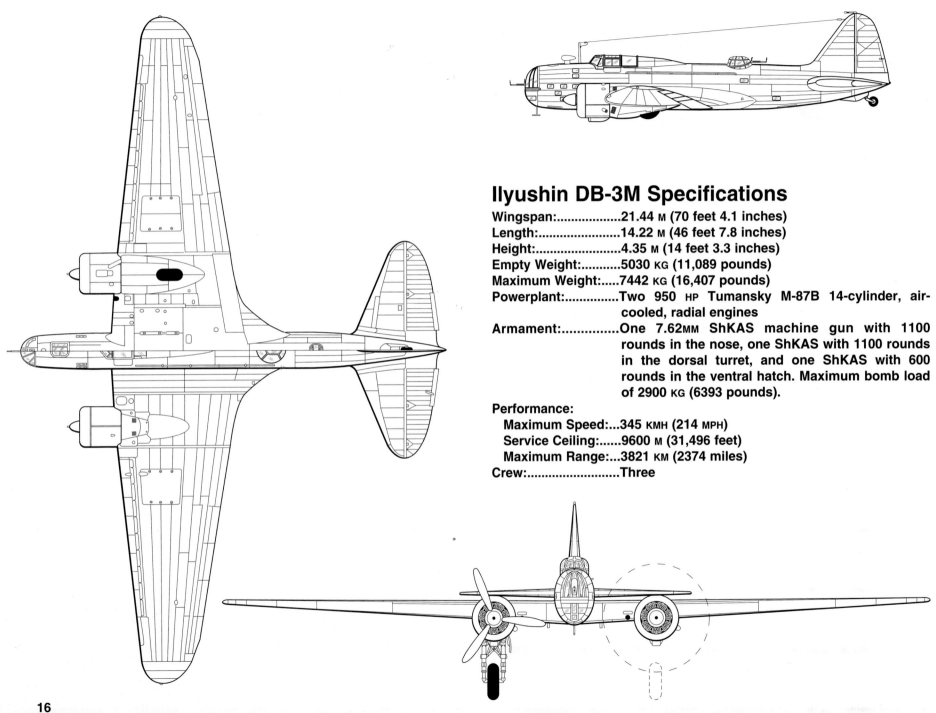

Ilyushin DB-3M Specifications

Wingspan:..................21.44 м (70 feet 4.1 inches)
Length:.......................14.22 м (46 feet 7.8 inches)
Height:.......................4.35 м (14 feet 3.3 inches)
Empty Weight:...........5030 KG (11,089 pounds)
Maximum Weight:.....7442 KG (16,407 pounds)
Powerplant:...............Two 950 HP Tumansky M-87B 14-cylinder, air-cooled, radial engines
Armament:...............One 7.62мм ShKAS machine gun with 1100 rounds in the nose, one ShKAS with 1100 rounds in the dorsal turret, and one ShKAS with 600 rounds in the ventral hatch. Maximum bomb load of 2900 KG (6393 pounds).

Performance:
  Maximum Speed:...345 KMH (214 MPH)
  Service Ceiling:.......9600 м (31,496 feet)
  Maximum Range:...3821 KM (2374 miles)
Crew:..........................Three

Two venturi tubes are mounted under the cockpit of this factory fresh DB-3M. A venturi tube collected airflow to either power vacuum instruments or measure airspeed. This bomber has full combat equipment, including three 7.62MM ShKAS machine guns. Pre-war DB-3s had national insignias on the wing upper surfaces. (Viktor Kulikov)

The DB-3M cockpit featured a centrally mounted control column and wheel for the pilot. Flight instruments are mounted on the panel immediately ahead of this wheel. Radio and oxygen equipment is mounted along the starboard cockpit wall.

nose. A number of DB-3Ms had a rear view mirror atop the cockpit frame. Late production aircraft had a retractable LUMV-2 gun mount on the lower rear gun position. The LUMV-2 was equipped with the 7.62MM ShKAS and provided an improved field of fire. Two side windows fitted to DM-3Ms with the LUMV-2 opened before retracting the mount.

A number of shortcomings became clear during DB-3M service operation. The aircraft lacked cabin heating and castor oil fumes caused nausea to the crew. Additionally, many instruments and equipment were in unsuitable locations. On the other hand, the aircraft had good handling characteristics. It easily made steep turns and was stable in level flight. The main difficulties were encountered during take off, where there was a tendency to laterally swing since both propellers rotated to port. There were cases of oil radiator freezing that led to overheated engines. The situation became worse when pilots opened the cowl flaps. It was necessary to close the radiator flaps, decelerate to a slower speed, and maintain the engines at 2000 RPM. Crews were ordered to abandon the aircraft if the oil radiators did not thaw.

In December of 1938, a service conference was held at Monino near Moscow. This meeting allowed the three *Vozdushnaya Armiya* (VAs; Air Armies) flying DB-3s to exchange information on their operating experiences. During two years of service, the DB-3 met the current tactical and technical requirements, but it was exceptionally complex to maintain and to operate. The DB-3 suffered a number of manufacturing defects on the fuel tank system and the undercarriage. Undercarriage failures caused three DB-3Ms to collapse during the summer of 1938.

The first DB-3M (Serial Number 39 23 20) fell into enemy hands on 29 January 1940, during the Finnish-Soviet Winter War. This aircraft subsequently saw service with the *Ilmavoimat* (Finnish Air Force), along with four more DB-3Ms captured during this conflict. The Finns loaned one aircraft (VP-13) to the German Luftwaffe, which was also interested in the DB-3. This DB-3M flew to the Luftwaffe's Test and Evaluation Center at Rechlin on 12 May 1941, six weeks before the German invasion of the Soviet Union. The aircraft was used for several trials at Rechlin before the Germans returned it to Finland on 12 September 1941.

Squadron Leader C.E. Slee of the British mission in Moscow flew a DB-3M from Kratovo airfield on 15 October 1941. He found the controls were heavy and the brakes were not up to British standards, but Slee praised its easy taxiing and the good view from the cockpit.

Three State Aviation Factories – GAZ 39 (Moscow-Khodinka), 18 (Voronezh), and 126 (Komsomolsk-na-Amur) – built 1103 DB-3s. GAZ 18 manufactured the DB-3 between 1937 and late 1938, while GAZ 126 continued with DB-3M production until 1941.

Both engines were controlled through the throttle mounted on the DB-3M's port cockpit side. The pilot could move both levers simultaneously, or each one individually. A compass is mounted to the cockpit wall ahead of the throttle. Fuel controls are located alongside the pilot's seat. Soviet aircraft interiors were usually painted Interior Gray (FS24226).

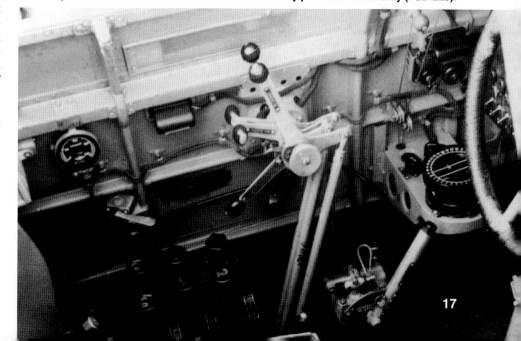

Finnish DB-3M

The first DB-3M (Serial Number 39 23 20) captured by the *Ilmavoimat* (Finnish Air Force) is parked in a hangar at Malmi, Finland on 3 March 1940. This aircraft was briefly operated in an overall natural metal finish before it was camouflaged. The fuselage code VP-101 was changed to VP-11 in December of 1940. (Klaus Niska)

This Finnish DB-3M (DB-13) was captured during the Soviet-Finnish Winter War of 1939-40. The bomber was sent to Rechlin, Germany for evaluation purposes on 12 May 1941. DB-13 was the last airworthy example in Finnish Air Force service and made its final flight on 1 November 1945. The aircraft is camouflaged with Olive Green and Black upper surfaces and Light Blue undersurfaces, with a Yellow aft fuselage band. (Klaus Niska)

Soviet forces attacked Finland on 30 November 1939, starting the Winter War. DB-3Ms of the 6th, 21st, and 53rd *Dal'nyi Bombardirovoch'nyi Aviatsion'nyi Polki* (DBAPs; Long-Range Bomber Aviation Regiments) and the 1st *Mino-Torpednaya Aviatsiya Polk* (MTAP; Mine-Torpedo Aviation Regiment) mounted operations on the conflict's first day. The Soviets quickly realized that the war against Finland was a complete disaster, which can be directly attributed to lack of adequate preparation and poor leadership. The latter was caused by Stalin's purges between 1937 and 1938, when half of the RKKA (Red Army) officer corps were shot. During the course of the hostilities, Finnish fighters, and especially the accurate anti-aircraft fire, caused heavy losses among the DB-3 regiments. Additionally, the poor training standard of the flight crews and equipment malfunctions were other adverse factors for the DB-3s. In early 1940, the 7th, 42nd, and 85th DBAPs joined the theater of operation. The Soviets lost over 50 DB-3 during three months and 13 days of combat.

During the Winter War, the Finns had captured five DB-3Ms that were repairable. The first DB-3M (Serial Number 39 23 20) 'Red 15' was taken intact at Hauho on 29 January 1940. This GAZ 39-built aircraft was given the *Ilmavoimat* serial VP-101 on 29 February 1940. The aircraft was lost after a crash landing at Lake Hirvaslampi following an engine failure on 30 June 1941.

The four other DB-3Ms captured in the Winter War required more than a year of repairs at the Air Depot at Tampere and were back in operation between February and June of 1941. These bombers were originally serialed VP-12 to VP-15, but the registration was changed from VP to DB in September of 1941. The numerical suffix remained unchanged. The Finns purchased six additional DB-3Ms from German war booty stocks. These bombers arrived in Finland on 12 September 1941 and were marked DB-16 to DB-21.

The Finns made several modifications to their DB-3s during their *Ilmavoimat* service. Entry handhold rails were mounted to both sides of the upper nose. Two landing lights were added to the starboard wing leading edge on most Finnish DB-3Ms. The Finns replaced the starboard opening nose entry hatch with an enlarged hatch that slid aft on rails. A few *Ilmavoimat* DB-3Ms had two bomb racks mounted under each wing. Four DB-3Ms (DB-17 to DB-20) had two small windows installed on both aft fuselage sides. DB-20 also had a large bulge built in the nose to house an RMK 20/30 x 30 camera. Another aircraft (DB-21) had its pitot head relocated from the underside nose to the portside nose section and a large venturi tube added on the port nose side. This tube was also installed on the first Finnish DB-3 (VP-11).

Ilmavoimat DB-3Ms were camouflaged with Black-Green (FS34050) and Olive Green (FS34096) upper surfaces and Light Blue (FS35414) undersurfaces. The aft fuselage band and undersurface wing wingtips were painted Yellow (FS33538) during Finland's Continuation War of 1941-44. These Yellow markings were overpainted after Finland switched to the Allies in the fall of 1944.

Finnish DB-3Ms were initially assigned to *Pommituslentolaivue* (PleLv; Bomber Squadron) 48 at Onttola for reconnaissance and bombing missions. On 2 June 1941, a DB-3 (VP-14) suffered an engine failure at 7500 м (24,606 feet), spin-dived into Lake Konnevsi, and exploded. Another DB-3 (DB-12) was lost during a crash landing on 19 August 1942. During an emergency landing of DB-18 on 17 September 1942, the bomb load exploded and the bomber was destroyed. DB-15 was written off during an emergency landing at Lake Pielinen on 20 February 1943. All four losses were due to technical malfunctions. PleLv 48's DB-3s flew 27 missions during the conflict with the Soviet Union.

In November of 1943, the seven remaining DB-3Ms were transferred to the 3rd Flight of LeLv (Flying Squadron) 46. They were assigned to bomb Soviet targets designated by Finnish Army Headquarters. DB-20 was lost in a take off accident on 29 February 1944. The DB-3Ms

The Finns purchased this DB-3M (DB-18) from German war booty stocks and it arrived in Finland on 12 September 1941. It has two windows added under the horizontal stabilizer and two landing lights on the wing leading edge. The insignia of LeLv (Flying Squadron) 48's 2nd Flight is painted on the nose. DB-18 was destroyed when it caught fire and its bomb load exploded during an emergency landing from Höytiäinen, Finland on 17 September 1942. (Klaus Niska)

of LeLv 46 flew 44 missions against Soviet targets, with the last on 8 August 1944. On 4 September 1944, Finland and the Soviet Union signed a truce agreement and Finland turned against the Germans. Yellow identification markings were painted over on the wing tips and fuselage. The *Ilmavoimat* lost only one DB-3 to German forces, when anti-aircraft fire hit DB-16 during a mission on 22 October 1944. The aircraft belly landed into marshland near

Soviet DB-3M

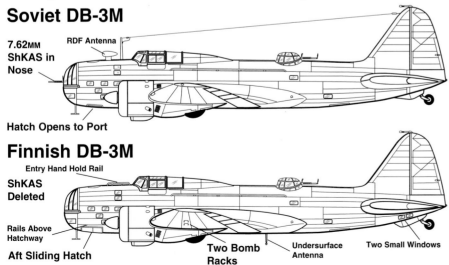

7.62MM ShKAS in Nose

RDF Antenna

Hatch Opens to Port

Finnish DB-3M

Entry Hand Hold Rail

ShKAS Deleted

Rails Above Hatchway

Aft Sliding Hatch

Two Bomb Racks

Undersurface Antenna

Two Small Windows

The Finns modified their DB-3Ms with a large venturi tube on the starboard nose above the center row of windows. This aircraft (DB-21) also has an aft sliding entrance hatch under the front fuselage, replacing the original Soviet entrance hatch. This DB-3M was purchased from German war booty stocks and survived World War Two. (Klaus Niska)

Ounasjoki, Lapland. DB-3Ms flew the last of 31 war missions against the Wehrmacht on 22 March 1945. Only four of Finland's 11 DB-3s survived the war. The last Finnish DB-3 (DB-13) was flown to a storage depot on 1 November 1945 after flying 372 hours in *Ilmavoimat* service.

The large bulge fitted under the nose of this Finnish Air Force DB-3 (DB-20) housed an RMK 20/30 x 30 camera. This particular aircraft has an antenna mast fitted ahead of the cockpit, unlike most Finnish DB-3s. DB-20 crashed on take off from Mensuvaara, Finland on 29 February 1944 and was written off. (Klaus Niska)

Ilyushin DB-3F Prototype

Kliment E. Voroshilov, the Commissar and chairman of the VVS (Soviet Air Force), ordered a dramatic increase in DB-3 production in 1938. The annual output of DB-3s at GAZ 39 at Moscow-Khodinka was to rise from 600 bombers to 1000 aircraft. Additionally, Voroshilov called for two new factories that would produce a total of 2500 DB-3s.

Ilyushin began a DB-3 modernization program in 1938. One of the program's two aims was to eliminate shortcomings in DB-3 production and handling characteristics, while increasing the aircraft's performance. The other objective was to redesign the airframe for increased mass production. This included replacing scarce dural (aluminum alloy) parts with components of either steel or wood.

Experiences in the three State Aviation Factories showed that DB-3 construction was highly complex and extremely time consuming. A number of workers could not properly master the modern manufacturing techniques, especially welding the wing components.

The Soviet Union lacked the knowledge of economically mass producing large all-metal aircraft in the late 1930s. Soviet designer Boris P. Lisunov and his staff stayed at the Douglas plant at Santa Monica, California between November of 1936 and December of 1939. Lisunov and his designers were engaged in the license building of the DC-3 airliner in the Soviet Union; however, they also studied the modern loft-and-pattern method, in which the DC-3 was assembled in large quantities in excellent quality. This production technique was quickly adopted on the DB-3. Together with the constructive improvements on the Ilyushin bomber, American production methods were also introduced to the State Aviation Factories.

The overall natural metal DB-3F prototype is parked during the Factory Test Trials held in the summer of 1939. This aircraft featured a simplified airframe for easier construction and a lengthened nose. A landing light is installed on the starboard wing leading edge, unlike the earlier DB-3M and later production DB-3F aircraft. (Viktor Kulikov)

The successor of the DB-3M is considered more as an entirely new design than a derivative of an existing model. The new type received the designation **DB-3F** (*forsirovannii*; forced or intensive). This designation was changed to Il-4 in March of 1942.

Most DB-3F changes were to the internal wing and fuselage structures. The whole DB-3F airframe was revised to the template assembly technology. All of the U-profiles and the minor welded joints were deleted. I-profile beams replaced the tubular spars and pressed parts replaced the small size ribs and bulkheads. Use of the I-profile beams eased production, saved time, and reduced the required work skills. Open two-sided riveting was employed for assembly, which allowed for open riveted joints that were easy to inspect.

The original welded tubular frames were retained in the engine mountings and a few other sections. The new assembling technology reduced the man-hours for completing a bomber from 30,301 hours on the DB-3M to 14,331 hours on the DB-3F.

Four self-sealing fuel cells in the inboard wing section and two integral tanks in the outboard wings replaced the ten integral fuel tanks. Total fuel capacity increased from 2860 L (756 gallons) in the DB-3B to 3855 L (1018 gallons) in the DB-3F. This new variant also had provision for fuel dumping in case of an emergency. The DB-3F prototype was equipped with an American Sperry autopilot acting on three axes (roll, pitch, and yaw); however, this device was not fitted on early production DB-3Fs.

The most prominent external modification was a fuselage lengthened from 14.22 м (46 feet 7.8 inches) on the DB-3M to 14.79 м (48 feet 6.3 inches) on the DB-3F. The nose section was completely redesigned and extensively glazed. A glazed nose compartment entry hatch replaced the solid nose compartment entry hatch. The DB-3F did not have the rear view mirror mounted atop the canopy frame as on several DB-3Ms.

Although the wing span remained at 21.44 м (70 feet 4.1 inches), the wing area increased from 65.6 м² (706 square feet) in the DB-3 to 66.7 м² (718 square feet) in the DB-3F. This was accomplished through an increased flap area. The single circular oil cooler inlet inboard of the wing leading edge was replaced by two circular intakes outboard of the engine. The DB-3F prototype deleted the DB-3M's provision for wing bomb racks. The DB-3 did not have any landing lights, but the DB-3F prototype had a light in both port and starboard wing leading

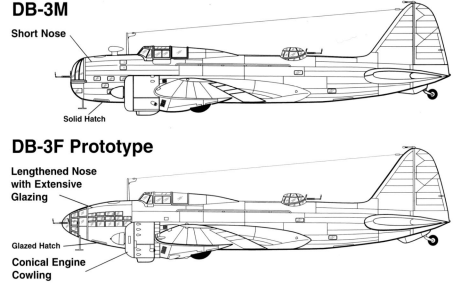

DB-3M

Short Nose

Solid Hatch

DB-3F Prototype

Lengthened Nose
with Extensive
Glazing

Glazed Hatch

Conical Engine
Cowling

The M-88 engine-equipped DB-3F prototype is parked during the Factory Test Trials in mid-1939. It retained the DB-3M's flat MV-3 upper fuselage turret. Standard production DB-3Fs were equipped with a bubble shaped version of the MV-3 turret. The DB-3F prototype carried a single position light on the wing tip, while production aircraft had two position lights on the upper and lower wing tips. (Viktor Kulikov)

edges.

A rear gunner for the dorsal turret was added to the crew, which was increased from three men on earlier DB-3s to four on the DB-3F. The radio operator manned the ventral machine gun. The navigator-bombardier in the lengthened nose had auxiliary flight controls to fly the aircraft if the pilot was incapacitated.

The DB-3's complex and collapse-prone undercarriage was simplified on the DB-3F. The oleo shock absorber's travel was increased and both oleo legs were connected with X-shaped booms, which replaced the single-boom oleo leg attachments on the DB-3. The hydraulic retraction system was replaced by a pneumatic mechanism. Main gear tire diameter was increased from 80 CM (31.5 inches) to 100 CM (39.4 inches) and more effective brakes were installed in the wheels. The main gear cover doors were flush on the DB-3M, but two blisters were fitted on the DB-3F wheel cover doors to accommodate the larger tires.

Power for the DB-3F prototype was supplied by two new M-88 engines, each with a take off output of 1100 HP. The M-88 was derived from the M-87 and developed by Sergei K. Tumansky and his KB (Design Bureau). The first M-88 became available in 1939. The DB-3M's VISh-3 three-bladed propeller was replaced on the DB-3F by the VISh-23.

The engine cowling was also modified, with the two upper exhaust stacks and the exhaust grills behind the lower main exhaust stack deleted. The front cowling section became more conical and several teardrop-shaped blisters were added on the nacelle panel. One larger exhaust stack replaced the two smaller stacks mounted on the cowling's starboard side. One carburetor inlet was mounted atop the engine cowling.

Vladimir K. Kokkinaki piloted the DB-3F prototype on its maiden flight on 21 May 1939. The three-month long flight development program revealed several defects in the aircraft. The M-88 proved extremely unreliable and was not fit for series production. The smaller cowlings led to a frequent engine overheating and the VISh-23 propellers frequently failed. The DB-3F prototype was retrofitted with more reliable M-87B engines turning VISh-3 propellers for the State Acceptance Trials, which began on 31 August 1939. The DB-3F prototype had a normal take off weight of 7660 KG (16,887 pounds) and attained 445 KMH (277 MPH) at 5400 M (17,717 feet) during these trials.

The DB-3F was originally powered by the new M-88 14-cylinder radial engine. This engine proved unreliable and was later replaced by the M-87B. Two lower exhaust stacks were mounted on the port and starboard nacelle sides. Two circular oil cooler intakes on the wing leading edge were typical for the DB-3F prototype and early production aircraft. The triangle-shaped fairing on the main landing gear door was typical on DB-3Fs, due to the fitting of larger tires. (Viktor Kulikov)

Upper cowling panels are removed to reveal the DB-3F's M-88 engine. This powerplant had a take off output of 1100 HP, which was 150 HP more than on the M-87B. During factory trials held in the summer of 1941, the M-88 proved extremely unreliable. M-87s replaced M-88s on the DB-3F for the State Acceptance Trials. (Viktor Kulikov)

Ilyushin DB-3F (1939)

Gosudarstvennyi Aviatsionnyi Zavod (GAZ; State Aviation Factory) 39 *Imeni Menzhinskogo* at Moscow-Khodinka delivered the first batch of five DB-3Fs to the *Voyenno-Vozdushniye Sily* (VVS; Military Air Forces) in November of 1939. The VVS rejected all five aircraft due to severe technical defects. Many brand new M-88 engines delivered from GAZ 29 at Zaporozhe showed major defects. For this reason, M-87B engines were installed on most DB-3Fs on the production lines at GAZ 18 at Voronezh and GAZ 39. There was no external difference between M-87B-powered and M-88-powered DB-3Fs. The VVS rejected 29 of the 49 DB-3Fs delivered in December of 1939, due to engine and undercarriage defects.

Several features distinguished the DB-3F prototype and subsequent production aircraft. The landing light on the starboard wing leading edge was deleted on production DB-3Fs. Two position lights – one each on the upper and lower wing tip – replaced the DB-3F prototype's single wingtip position light. The lights were red to port and green to starboard. The two blisters on the main wheel cover doors were reduced in size, while production DB-3Fs had drop-shaped front blisters.

Production DB-3Fs were equipped with an enlarged version of the MV-3 rear upper fuselage turret. This replaced the flat shaped MV-3 turret on the DB-3F prototype. All DB-3F produced until the spring of 1940 lacked camouflage. National markings were painted on the upper and lower wing surfaces and the rear fuselage. Shortly before the Great Patriotic War began on 22 June 1941, Soviet *Dal'nyi Bombardirovoch'nyi Aviatsion'nyi Polki* (DBAPs; Long-Range Bomber Aviation Regiments) were ordered to camouflage the DB-3F's natural metal upper surfaces with green splotches. In most cases, these splotches were crudely applied by hand.

Early production DB-3Fs were delivered in natural metal finish in late 1939. The Wehrmacht (German forces) captured this aircraft (Yellow 11) during Germany's invasion of the Soviet Union (Operation BARBAROSSA) in June of 1941. The new MV-3 dorsal turret had a larger dome and reduced framing for better visibility. (George Punka)

Ilyushin DB-3F (1940)

Severe problems with the totally unreliable M-88 engine continued in early 1940. In the first quarter of that year, GAZ 29 delivered approximately 100 engines with major defects, which could not be installed in DB-3Fs. Additionally, defective oil coolers manufactured at GAZ 34 in Moscow were a constant problem. Many DB-3Fs suffered unacceptably high engine temperatures and oil leaks at altitude. These factors kept their production numbers low in early 1940.

Modifications to the M-88-powered DB-3F's oil cooling system continued until March of 1940. Simultaneously, the airframe underwent extensive modifications. From the original 8147 drawings drawn for the DB-3F prototype, 2174 new drawings were required and 5211 drawings were revised.

In January of 1940, GAZ 18 at Voronezh built nine DB-3Fs with M-87B engines and two DB-3Fs with M-88s. During the factory test trials, four M-88s had to be changed on four DB-3Fs due to oil spillage from breathers and engine component fractures during ground test runs. Broken piston rings were detected on M-88s in February of 1940. This happened before the engines were first test run. Intensive work was needed to eradicate these defects. GAZ 18 received notifications for 101 changes to the DB-3F design in late 1939 and 44 more changes, with many amendments issued to these changes, given by mid-March of 1940.

These changes included relocating the oil radiators along the forward wing spar. The two circular air intakes on the wing leading edge were replaced by a single, rectangular air intake. The DB-3F was equipped with ribbed wheel discs and brakes in the fall of 1940. These wheels were similar to those of the Junkers Ju-88K-1 and Dornier Do-215B-3, which the Soviets purchased from Germany in May of 1940. That October, a DB-3F was equipped with a thermal de-icing system copied from the Ju-88K-1.

GAZ 29 produced 850 M-88s by 1 June 1940; however, production was halted due to manufacturing defects on 11 June. The M-88's lack of reliability resulted in M-87Bs going into most DB-3Fs built in 1940. Additionally, the M-88 had a much greater specific fuel consumption than on the M-87. This resulted in M-88-powered DB-3Fs having a reduced range. The State Acceptance Program demonstrated the M-88-powered DB-3F was approximately 22 KMH (13.7 MPH) slower than the DB-3F equipped with the M-87B.

DB-3F Prototype

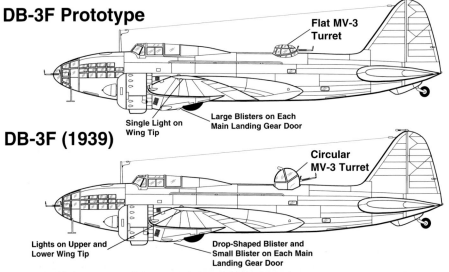

Flat MV-3 Turret

Single Light on Wing Tip

Large Blisters on Each Main Landing Gear Door

DB-3F (1939)

Circular MV-3 Turret

Lights on Upper and Lower Wing Tip

Drop-Shaped Blister and Small Blister on Each Main Landing Gear Door

Slovak troops stand before an early DB-3F destroyed by retreating Soviet forces in the summer of 1941. This aircraft has the two circular inlets mounted on the wing leading edge beside the engine. These inlets were typical on early production DB-3Fs. (Zdenek Hurt)

Three Slovak soldiers pose before a sabotaged early DB-3F in the western Soviet Union in mid-1941. A GAZ (State Aviation Factory) delivered this aircraft to the VVS (Soviet Air Force) in natural metal finish in late 1939. Green patches were crudely painted over the upper surfaces in the summer of 1941. This Soviet measure was intended to partially camouflage the aircraft while on the ground. (Zdenek Hurt)

Another important factor in improving the DB-3F was its armament development. It was realized that in the haste applied to the aircraft's development that several aspects were omitted. In contrast to the DB-3M, the DB-3F was unable to carry the 50-kg (110 pound) ZAB-50 incendiary bomb and the KhAB-25 and KRAB-25 chemical agent bombs.

On 23 May 1940, the VVS ordered DB-3Fs to be camouflaged light green on the upper surfaces and light blue on the undersurfaces. The red star national marking with thin black outline was placed on the upper and lower wing surfaces and the rear fuselage sides. Two days after the order had been issued, the first camouflaged DB-3Fs left the assembly lines.

Three State Aviation Factories completed 1006 DB-3Fs in 1940. These included 808 aircraft

built at GAZ 18 (Voronezh) and 198 DB-3Fs at GAZ 39 (Moscow-Khodinka). GAZ 126 at Komsomolsk-na-Amur continued to build the earlier DB-3M.

A DB-3F without defensive armament flies during a factory test flight in 1940. DB-3Fs were camouflaged with Light Green upper surfaces and Light Blue undersurfaces from late May of 1940. National markings – black-edged red stars – were painted on the rear fuselage and the wing upper and lower surfaces. (Viktor Kulikov)

Engine Intake and Exhaust Stack Development
Il-4 (1939)   Il-4 (1940)

Short Exhaust Stack

Two Protruding Intakes

Long Exhaust Stack

Single Flush Inlet

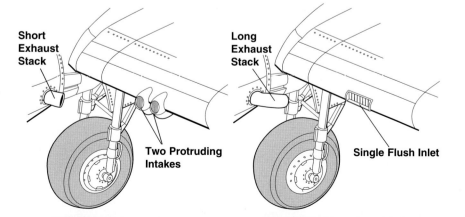

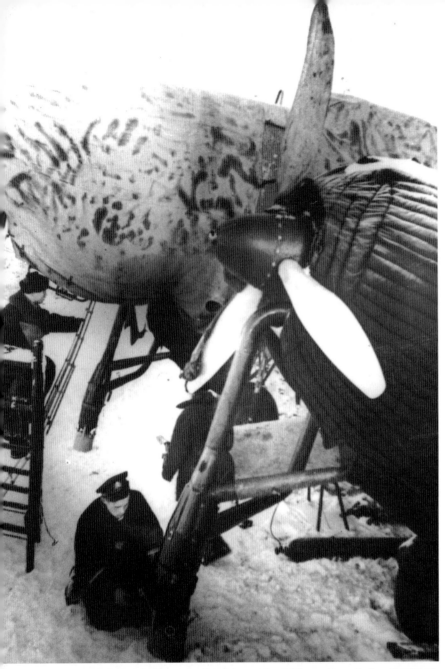

A winter camouflaged DB-3F (Red 37) prepares to take off for another mission. White painted upper surfaces allowed the aircraft to blend in with the snow-covered landscape. No national markings were placed on the white upper surfaces of this DB-3F. Undersurfaces retained their Light Blue finish to match the sky. Newly built DB-3Fs were factory-painted in this camouflage during the Winter months. (Viktor Kulikov)

This early DB-3F could not be flown away when German forces overran the airfield. The DB-3F had larger flaps than earlier DB-3s. These allowed for improved take off and landing characteristics at higher aircraft weights and speeds. The enlarged flaps increased the wing area from the DB-3's 65.6 M^2 (706 square feet) to 66.7 M^2 (718 square feet) on the DB-3F. The cowlings were removed to reveal the M-87B engines. (RART)

Gas-operated burners were used to pre-heat the engines during the harsh winter months. One burner supplied heated air to an engine and its carburetor air intake prior to starting the engine. Canvas covers are fitted over the engine cowling and the nose. One crewman used a ladder to enter the nose compartment through a hatch in the lower nose section.

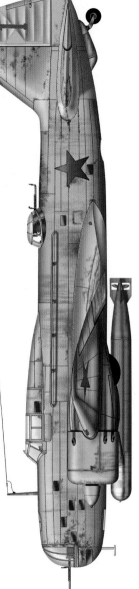

This Ilyushin DB-3T (Red 1) was assigned to a VVS VMF (Soviet Naval Aviation) regiment in the 1938-41 period. The overall Light Gray (approximately FS36622) aircraft is armed with one 45-CM (17.7-inch) Type 45-36-AN torpedo under the fuselage.

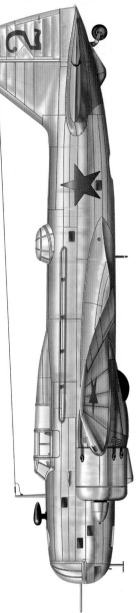

Blue 2 was an early production DB-3M assigned to a Long-Range Aviation Regiment of the Soviet VVS (Air Force). It is left in overall natural metal. An air data boom is mounted on the nose.

Finnish forces captured this DB-3M during the 1939-40 Winter War and assigned the serial DB-13 to this aircraft. A black moose personal insignia is painted on the tail. The Finns loaned this DB-3M to the German Luftwaffe for evaluation purposes in May of 1941.

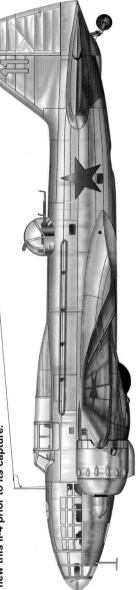

The Germans captured this early Il-4 (Yellow 11) in the summer of 1941. Early production DB-3Fs (Il-4s) were delivered in natural metal. A Mine-Torpedo Aviation Regiment of the VVS KBF (Red Banner Baltic Fleet Air Force) flew this Il-4 prior to its capture.

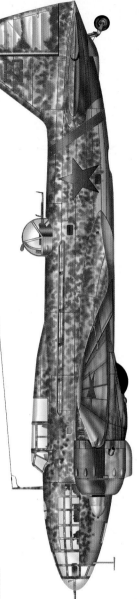

A crudely applied Dark Green (approx. FS34092) upper surface camouflage was painted on this Il-4 (Red 23). This scheme was authorized for natural metal VVS aircraft during the summer of 1941. Retreating Soviet forces destroyed Red 23 to prevent its capture by advancing Axis forces.

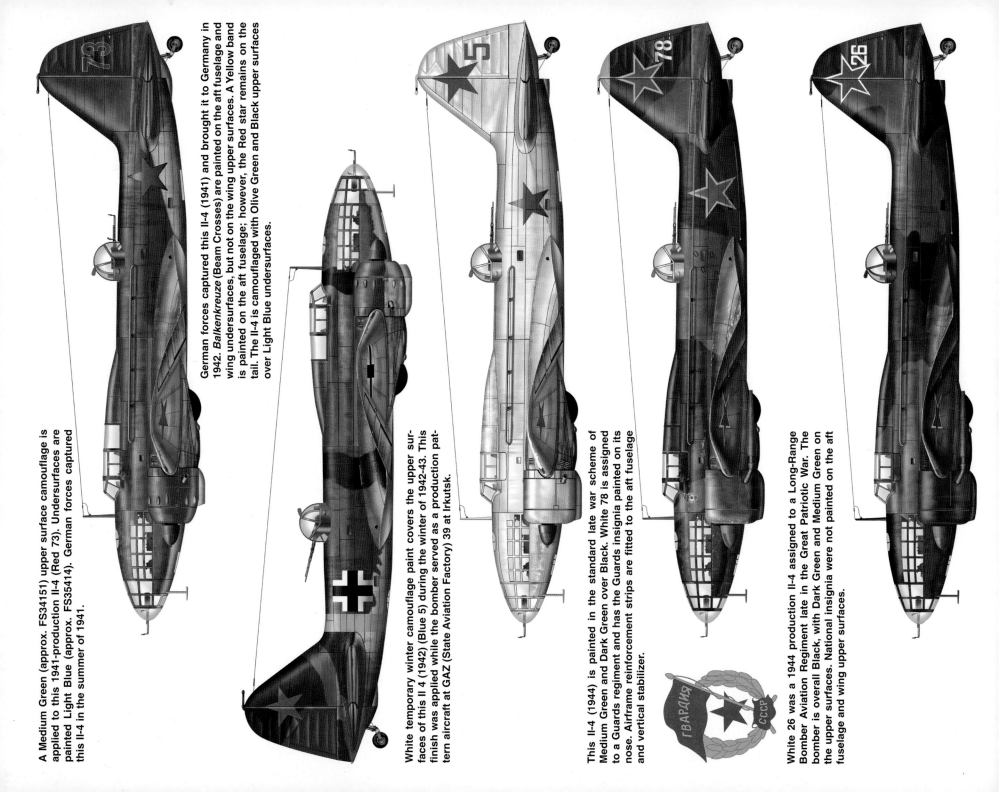

A Medium Green (approx. FS34151) upper surface camouflage is applied to this 1941-production Il-4 (Red 73). Undersurfaces are painted Light Blue (approx. FS35414). German forces captured this Il-4 in the summer of 1941.

German forces captured this Il-4 (1941) and brought it to Germany in 1942. *Balkenkreuze* (Beam Crosses) are painted on the aft fuselage and wing undersurfaces, but not on the wing upper surfaces. A Yellow band is painted on the aft fuselage; however, the Red star remains on the tail. The Il-4 is camouflaged with Olive Green and Black upper surfaces over Light Blue undersurfaces.

White temporary winter camouflage paint covers the upper surfaces of this Il 4 (1942) (Blue 5) during the winter of 1942-43. This finish was applied while the bomber served as a production pattern aircraft at GAZ (State Aviation Factory) 39 at Irkutsk.

This Il-4 (1944) is painted in the standard late war scheme of Medium Green and Dark Green over Black. White 78 is assigned to a Guards regiment and has the Guards insignia painted on its nose. Airframe reinforcement strips are fitted to the aft fuselage and vertical stabilizer.

White 26 was a 1944 production Il-4 assigned to a Long-Range Bomber Aviation Regiment late in the Great Patriotic War. The bomber is overall Black, with Dark Green and Medium Green on the upper surfaces. National insignia were not painted on the aft fuselage and wing upper surfaces.

Ilyushin DB-3F (1941)/Il-4 (1942)

The DB-3F's many shortcomings and the urgent need for both Petlyakov Pe-2 dive-bombers and Il-2 Shturmovik assault aircraft ended DB-3F production at GAZ 18 (Voronezh) in April of 1941. GAZ 39 (Moscow-Khodinka) halted DB-3F production soon afterward. This left GAZ 126 (Komsomolsk-na-Amur) as the only factory building the DB-3F. The VVS briefly considered halting DB-3F production in favor of the twin-engine DB-240 (later Yer-2) developed by Vladimir G. Yermolayev; however, the Soviets halted Yer-2 production.

Apart from its severe technical shortcomings, the DB-3F was far from an ideal aircraft for maintenance. The DB-3F took longer to maintain compared to Junkers Ju-88K-1 purchased from Germany in May of 1940. It took 15 minutes to remove a propeller spinner from the DB-3F, compared to only five seconds on the Ju-88K-1. An engine installation that required three hours on the Ju-88 K-1 took 12 hours on the DB-3F.

A new larger diameter engine cowling had been fitted in mid 1941. This was done to overcome engine overheating problems. The drop shaped blisters were deleted, a straight front section replaced the original conical section, and the carburetor air intake tunnel was enlarged. The centerline intake atop the engine cowling was reduced in size, while the lower exhaust stack had been enlarged. A small squared window was added to the nose section's upper window row.

After the Great Patriotic War began on 22 June 1941, DB-3Fs were painted a two-tone upper surface camouflage of Medium Green and Black Green. National markings were placed on the rear fuselage and the lower wing surfaces, but not on the upper wing surfaces. The original Light Blue undersurfaces were overpainted Flat Black when the DBAPs (Long-Range Bomber Aviation Regiments) began night operations.

DB-3Fs produced in the second half of 1941 had the rear canopy glazing replaced by a sheet metal part. The large tail wheel section fairing was deleted on DB-3Fs built in late 1941. These aircraft had a small fairing in front of the tail wheel strut. Most of the 757 DB-3Fs completed in 1941 were built at GAZ 126 at Komsomolsk-na-Amur.

The *Gosudarstennyy Komitet Oborony* (GKO; State Defense Committee) issued a resolution on 26 March 1942. This stated that the DB-3F was to be redesignated the Il-4 in honor of its designer, Sergei V. Ilyushin.

In the spring of 1942, the MV-3 dorsal turret with one 7.62MM ShKAS machine gun was replaced by a similar appearing UTK-1 turret carrying one 12.7MM Berezin UBT machine gun with 500 rounds of ammunition. The gunner in the UTK-1 turret was protected by armor plating between 6MM and 9MM thick.

The UBT weighed 21.5 KG (47.4 pounds), had a muzzle velocity of 860 M (2822 feet) per second, and a firing rate of 1000 rounds per minute. Equivalent figures for the 10.6 KG (23.4 pound) ShKAS were 825 M (2707 feet) per second muzzle velocity and 1800 rounds per minute firing rate. The UBT fired a 48 gram (1.7 ounce) bullet, which was three times heavier than the ShKAS's 16 gram (0.6 ounce) projectile. The improved range and striking power was more effective against German fighters.

In the fall of 1942, AV-5-F-158 propellers had replaced the VISh-3s and the flap area was increased by 2 M² (21.5 square feet). These improvements allowed for safer operation from poor quality airfields. A thicker airflow section on the wing tips and a shift of the lower rib strips enabled an increase from one to three self-sealing fuel tanks in the outer wing panels, increasing the fuel capacity from 2860 L (756 gallons) to 3855 L (1018 gallons).

State Aviation Factories built 858 Il-4s in 1942. Output of this bomber was low compared to that of the Pe-2 and the Il-2. The VVS gave priority to ground attack aircraft and medium dive-bombers at this stage of the conflict. Additionally, the Il-4's all metal construction greatly consumed scarce resources. North American B-25 Mitchells supplied by the US under the Lend-Lease program were assigned to the DBAPs. These compensated for the low Il-4 production rate.

This DB-3F was equipped with skis placed around the main landing gear wheels. These wooden skis eased taxiing over snow-covered airfields and were jettisoned upon take off. The aircraft is painted White on the upper surfaces and Black on the undersurfaces. National markings were oversprayed on the wing undersurfaces, whose Black finish camouflaged the aircraft at night. The Soviets redesignated the DB-3F as the Il-4 on 26 March 1942. (Viktor Kulikov)

DB-3F (1940)

MV-3 Turret with 7.62MM ShKAS

Rear Canopy Glazing

Conical Cowling with Small Carburetor Inlet

Large Tail Wheel Fairing

Il-4 (1941-42)

UTK-1 Turret with 12.7MM UBT

Rear Glazing Deleted

Large Diameter Cowling with Large Carburetor Inlet

Small Tail Wheel Fairing

This DB-3F has additional reinforcing strips installed on the wing undersurfaces. This configuration was never adopted in series production. This particular DB-3F lacks the squared window placed normally on the upper window row. The radio compass antenna is located in a teardrop-shaped fairing on the lower nose. (Viktor Kulikov)

This DB-3F is equipped with a flatter windscreen than on standard production aircraft. The glazed rear canopy was typical for early DB-3Fs (Il-4s), but the bomber is equipped with the late production engine cowlings. (Viktor Kulikov)

Several winter camouflaged DB-3Fs are lined up at an airfield prior to a mission. The original Green upper surface camouflage is retained in front of the cockpit. Flat Black undersurfaces were first used when the VVS began reassigning DB-3Fs from day to night missions. (RART)

Crewmen of a DB-3F (Red 3) prepare for a mission in the Black Sea region. This bomber was assigned to a Guards Regiment of the VVS ChF (Black Sea Fleet Air Force). Weathering of the black and green upper surface camouflage reveals rivets used to bond the skin to the framing. UTK-1 turret frames were left in natural metal. (RART)

Ilyushin Il-4 (1943/1945)

At the beginning of 1943, the Il-4 was produced at GAZ 23 at Fili, GAZ 81 at Moscow-Tushino, and GAZ 126 at Komsomolsk-na-Amur. Petlyakov Pe-3 and Pe-3*bis* fighter production at GAZ 39 at Irkutsk gave way to Il-4 construction in March of 1943. The Irkutsk plant delivered 698 Il-4s by year's end. Improvements on all production lines led to a more economical production of the bomber. At the beginning of the DB-3F production in November of 1939, assembling one DB-3F required 14,331 man-hours. This figure was dropped to 12,500 man-hours in 1943, indicating that the heavy Il-4 bomber required fewer man-hours to produce than Pe-2 medium bombers.

M-88 engine problems were fully solved by this time and all subsequent Il-4s were equipped with this engine. The later M-88B had the same output as the M-88, but was improved in details. During the harsh winter conditions, engine cowling louvers were fitted in front of the engine cylinders.

Strengthened main wheels were fitted to Il-4s from early 1943. Simultaneously, the tail-wheel's dimensions were increased from 400MM (15.7 inches) in diameter by 150MM (5.9 inches) wide to 470MM (18.5 inches) by 210MM (8.3 inches).

The Il-4 was equipped with a de-icing system, which used heated air passed from heat exchangers on the exhaust stacks to the wing leading edges. Separate heat sources served the tail surfaces. A de-icing liquid was sprayed across the flight deck windshield. Heat exchangers slightly reduced the aircraft's speed, but this increased the range of operations in adverse weather conditions. An 8MM armored backrest was fitted to the navigator's seat, while the pilot had 13MM armor plating on his cockpit's aft bulkhead.

The APG-1 Automatic Direction Finder (ADF) was installed in every second Il-4 built from mid-1943. Ultraviolet (UV) instrument panel lights for night flying were standard equipment at this time. These lights were previously fitted at the unit level. The SPU-4F intercom system replaced the earlier SPU-3 in the summer of 1943, while an improved oxygen system was installed. The main wheels had been enlarged to 1100MM (43.3 inches) in diameter by 400MM (15.7 inches) wide. In mid-1943, four reinforcing strips were attached to the rear fuselages of Il-4s. Two strips each were fitted to the upper and lower fuselage. Additionally, an external reinforcing strip was fitted above the horizontal stabilizer on each side.

The increased deployment of Il-4s in night bombing missions resulted in the development of exhaust flame dampers at the Regiment and Division levels. Most of these field-developed dampers proved less effective in service. The *Tsentral'noe Institut Aviatsionnogo Motorostroeniyua* (TsIAM; Central Institute of Aircraft Engines) responded by developing the GAM-9 flame damper, which featured a cooling air tube over the exhaust stack. This modification lengthened the Il-4's exhaust stack compared to the standard stack.

The new 1250 HP M-88V engine became available for Il-4s in the fall of 1943. This radial engine had a 150 HP increase in output compared to the previous M-88B, while the Time Between Overhauls (TBO) increased from 100 hours of operation to 200 hours. Dust filters were fitted to the engine air intakes. State Aviation Factories built 1558 Il-4s in 1943. Fully feathered UF-611F propellers became standard on Il-4s built from October of 1944.

Most *Aviatsiya Dal'niya Destviya* (ADD; Long-Range Aviation)[1] Il-4s were delivered in a three-tone upper surface camouflage of Medium Green (approximately FS34151), Dark Green (approx. FS34092), and Black (FS37038). Some aircraft were painted with Dark Green and Medium Green upper surfaces. All these Il-4s had Flat Black undersurfaces. National insignias were now painted only on the vertical tail and lower wing surfaces. A large white border and a thin red outline were added to the national insignia from early 1944.

In early 1945, the improved AV-7E-158A propeller replaced the UF-611F propeller on production Il-4s. Some aircraft were equipped with a solid nose compartment hatch with a rectangular window, which replaced the fully glazed hatch of earlier Il-4s.

Il-4 production at the Voronezh facility – now designated GAZ 64 – resumed in early 1945. This factory assembled aircraft from sub-assemblies sent by other plants. Il-4 production at Voronezh continued until late 1945, when GAZ 64 began retooling to produce the Il-10 assault aircraft.

Avionics were not standardized, even in the final stage of Il-4 production. Available equipment included the AVP-2 autopilot, the APG-1 Automatic Direction Finder (ADF), the *Noch-*

[1]ADD: This became the 18th *Vozdushnaya Armiya* (VA; Air Army) on 16 December 1944

Several highly weathered Il-4s assemble for take off. Harsh climactic conditions and the inferior quality of Soviet paint combined to cause wear on the Il-4's paint scheme. Both aircraft in the foreground have natural metal cockpit canopy framing and each Il-4's navigator leans out through the upper nose hatch. (Viktor Kulikov)

Il-4 (1941-42)

M-87B Engines

Il-4 (1943)

M-88/M-88B Engines

Reinforcing Strips on Aft Fuselage and Tail

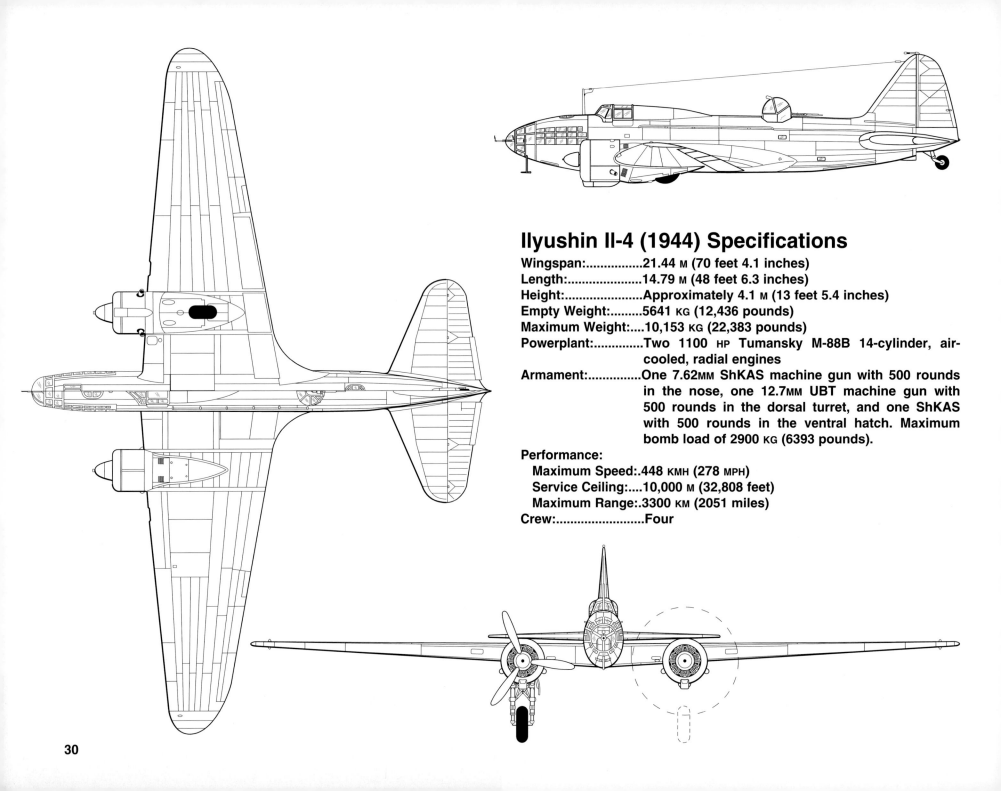

Ilyushin Il-4 (1944) Specifications

Wingspan:................21.44 м (70 feet 4.1 inches)
Length:....................14.79 м (48 feet 6.3 inches)
Height:....................Approximately 4.1 м (13 feet 5.4 inches)
Empty Weight:.........5641 кG (12,436 pounds)
Maximum Weight:....10,153 кG (22,383 pounds)
Powerplant:..............Two 1100 HP Tumansky M-88B 14-cylinder, air-cooled, radial engines
Armament:...............One 7.62MM ShKAS machine gun with 500 rounds in the nose, one 12.7MM UBT machine gun with 500 rounds in the dorsal turret, and one ShKAS with 500 rounds in the ventral hatch. Maximum bomb load of 2900 кG (6393 pounds).
Performance:
  Maximum Speed:.448 кMH (278 MPH)
  Service Ceiling:....10,000 м (32,808 feet)
  Maximum Range:.3300 кM (2051 miles)
Crew:........................Four

Il-4s assigned to the 119th Naval Reconnaissance Aviation Regiment prepare for a mission in June of 1943. They are equipped with the short exhaust stacks, which were standard before GAM-9 flame dampers were introduced. The Il-4s have Dark Green, Medium Green, and Black upper surfaces and Black undersurfaces. National markings are not painted on the aft fuselage. (Viktor Kulikov)

Workers complete assembly of an Il-4 just rolled out of GAZ (State Aviation Factory) 64 at Voronezh in early 1945. This factory assembled Il-4s from components delivered from other Soviet factories. The starboard main wheel is missing, although the port wheel is installed. National insignia are painted on the aft fuselage and fin, but not on the wing upper surfaces. (Vladimir Gagin)

1 Instrument Landing System (ILS) unit, and the RPK-2 direction finding device. Most late production Il-4s had the RSB-3*bis* radio.

The Il-4 formed the backbone of the DBAPs (Long-Range Bomber Aviation Regiments) during the Great Patriotic War. US-built B-25 Mitchell bombers supplied under Lend-Lease supplemented the Il-4s. The Il-4 had a better range and ceiling than the B-25, while the Mitchell boasted a 110 кмн (68 мрн) higher speed and greatly improved defensive armament over the Ilyushin aircraft. Many Soviet pilots preferred the Mitchell over the Il-4, because the American bomber had much greater instrumentation and more pleasing flying characteristics.

State Aviation Factories built 5256 Il-4s between November of 1939 and late 1945. This total included 2991 aircraft built at GAZ 126 at Komsomolsk-na-Amur. The Komsomolsk-na-Amur and Voronezh factories built 160 Il-4s after the end of World War Two. Some former bombers were converted into long-range photographic survey aircraft for the Ministry of Geology in 1946. All armament was deleted and photographic cameras were installed in the bomb bay.

The VVS began retiring the Il-4 from bombing service in 1947. The Soviet aircraft industry was beginning to master the complex production techniques necessary for building the Tupolev Tu-4 – the Soviet copy of the Boeing B-29 Superfortress bomber. The North Atlantic Treaty Organization's (NATO's) Air Standards Coordinating Committee (ASCC) assigned the reporting name Bob to the Il-4 in 1954 – two years after the Il-4 had left operational service.

A late production Il-4 (White 78) is seconds from take off on another mission. Il-4s began flying day missions after the Soviets gained air superiority over the Russian Front from mid-1943. The Guards insignia painted under the cockpit indicated the aircraft's assignments to a Guards unit. (Viktor Kulikov)

This Il-4 is equipped with the GAM-9 flame damper unit, which replaced the smaller flame damper previously used by these aircraft. The GAM-9 had improved flame-damping qualities over the earlier damper, yet allowed engine exhaust gases to efficiently vent from the aircraft. Short struts secured the GAM-9 to the nacelle.

An M-88-powered Il-4 is being refueled with 92-octane fuel supplied from a camouflaged fuel truck. Ground crews fully refueled an Il-4 in 45 minutes. This particular aircraft has a solid nose compartment hatch, with a window in the center. Two venturi tubes are mounted under the windshield on the starboard side. (RART)

An early flame damper is fitted to this Il-4's exhaust stack. The damper hid exhaust flames, which gave the bomber's position away at night. Il-4 main landing gears employed a single wheel with tire and retracted aft into its bay in the nacelle. Two oleo (shock absorbing) struts replaced the single oleo strut fitted to the earlier DB-3, while the Il-4 replaced the earlier aircraft's hydraulic gear operation with a pneumatic system.

Technicians perform light maintenance on a 1st MTAP (Mine-Torpedo Aviation Regiment) Il-4 between missions in 1944. This bomber has the standard highly glazed lower nose hatch. The 7.62MM ShKAS machine gun has been removed from its nose mount. A pitot tube for measuring airspeed is mounted on the nose's port side.

The nose-mounted ShKAS machine gun was equipped with a single ring sight. The 128-CM (50.4 inch) long machine gun weighed 10.6 KG (23.4 pounds) and was fitted to most Soviet aircraft of the Great Patriotic War. This 7.62MM weapon had a muzzle velocity of 825 M (2707 feet) per second and a firing rate of 1800 rounds per minute.

The ShKAS is mounted in the nose of this Il-4, which appears to be painted overall Light Gray. Three rows of five rectangular windows are placed on each side of the nose. These windows gave the navigator-bombardier visibility to both port and starboard. Additional windows are located immediately aft of the clear nose cone.

The navigator-bombardier operated the Il-4's nose-mounted ShKAS. Ammunition was fed from a 500-round box in the nose compartment to the weapon's breech. Spent cartridges were collected in a bag clipped to the gun's port side.

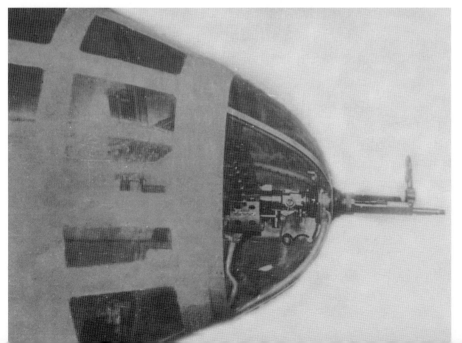

Weapons release controls and navigation instruments are fitted to the port side of the navigator-bombardier's compartment. Toggle switches on the control panel operated the bomb bay doors and to release bombs either in salvo or simultaneously. Il-4 navigator-bombardiers had basic flight controls, which enabled them to fly the aircraft if the pilot was incapacitated. (Viktor Kulikov)

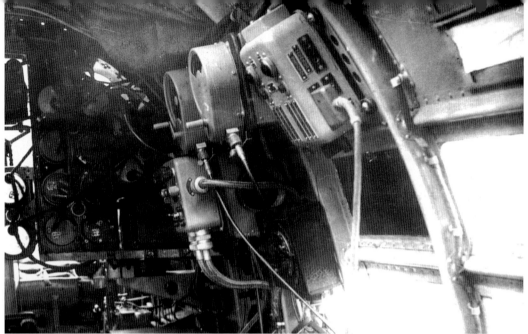

Intercom and oxygen controls are mounted along the port side of the navigator-bombardier compartment. Oxygen enabled crews to operate effectively at high altitude. The rear of the pilot's instrument panel is visible at the compartment's aft end. (Viktor Kulikov)

Oxygen bottles are mounted on the starboard side of the navigator-bombardier's compartment. A first aid kit is the large box on the compartment side above the bottles. Control cables for the pilot's and navigator-bombardier's throttles run down the nose compartment. The navigator-bombardier's padded seat is fitted to the floor, with a radio located to the seat's left. (Viktor Kulikov)

The Il-4's spartan instrument panel was similar to that of the earlier DB-3M. A pair of TE-22 tachometers are located on the upper left panel section, with two TME-41 oil and water temperature gauges placed immediately below. An AVR clock is fitted to the far port panel, while a KI-10 compass is located on the center. Most Il-4 instruments were copied from American flight gauges. (Viktor Kulikov)

Throttle levers are mounted along the port cockpit wall and are similar to those fitted to the DB-3M. Trim wheels located below the throttle quadrant adjusted the trim tabs mounted on the rudder, elevators, and ailerons. A compass is mounted along the cockpit wall ahead of the throttle. (Viktor Kulikov)

Three lights mounted atop the Il-4 instrument panel coaming guided the pilot during the bomb run. They indicated whether he was too far left, too far right, or in the exact position. Two engine air intake temperature gauges flank these lights. The navigator-bombardier's seat is located in the nose compartment through the aperture above the control column. (Viktor Kulikov)

Oxygen bottles for the forward crew members are mounted near the cockpit floor along the starboard wall. Radio and intercom equipment and controls are mounted along this wall. The oxygen control unit is mounted high along the wall near the instrument panel coaming. (Viktor Kulikov)

The RSB-bis radio is mounted in the Il-4's rear fuselage, immediately ahead of the MV-3 turret opening. This radio consisted of a transmitter on top and a receiver in the center. A distribution box with the RUK-300A and the RU-11A transformer is mounted below the receiver. (Viktor Kulikov)

A remotely controlled AFA-13 camera is mounted in the aft fuselage near the tail surfaces' leading edges. It was used to record the results of a bombing mission for post-strike analysis. The AFA-13 was also employed on reconnaissance missions. This camera weighed 13 KG (28.7 pounds) and took up to 150 photographs during one mission. (Viktor Kulikov)

The MV-3 dorsal turret's upper section opened to allow access for the turret gunner. The 7.62MM ShKAS machine gun normally mounted in this turret has been removed from this aircraft. A UTK-1 turret with a 12.7MM UBT replaced the MV-3 from mid-1942. Balance vanes on the turret reduced airflow pressure on the gun barrel. (Viktor Kulikov)

One 7.62MM ShKAS is mounted on a retractable LUMV-2 mount in the lower fuselage. Two windows opened when the weapon was deployed for firing. The radio operator usually fired the ShKAS, which moved 30° to both sides and 90° to the bottom. This weapon was supplied with 500 rounds of ammunition. (Viktor Kulikov)

The LUMV-2 ventral mount retracted into the lower fuselage and the two windows closed when combat was not expected. This ShKAS is equipped with an OP-2L periscope gun sight, which is fitted to the mount's upper frame. One of two flanking rectangular windows is located to port of the weapon. (Viktor Kulikov)

All Il-4s had a single fixed tail wheel, which was virtually the same as the tail wheel installed on DB-3s. A protective cover ahead of the wheel strut kept dirt and snow out of the aft fuselage. This cover was removed on later production Il-4s. (Viktor Kulikov)

DB-3F/II-4 in Combat

The DB-3 first saw combat in China in 1939, during the Sino-Japanese War. The Soviets delivered 24 DB-3Ms to the Chinese Air Force, which assigned these aircraft to its 8th Bomb Group and to a volunteer Soviet unit. Both units were based at Chengdu in the central province of Szechwan. The DB-3s flew a number of bombing missions against Japanese forces in eastern China. These included two successful raids on the Japanese airfield at Hankou (Hangzhou), located approximately 1500 KM (932 miles) from Chengdu. China's DB-3s were used until late 1943, when spare parts shortages and the availability of American-supplied bombers forced their retirement. No information is available regarding the numbers of DB-3s lost in combat and accidents during their Chinese service.

Soviet DB-3s were employed in the Winter War against Finland in 1939-40. Both the VVS (Air Force) and VMF (Navy) flew the Ilyushins on bombing missions against Finnish targets. A combination of factors – including poor training of DB-3 crews and strong Finnish defenses – resulted in heavy losses among Soviet DB-3 units.

The ADD had 1122 DB-3s and DB-3Fs – including 906 serviceable machines – in the Western Military District when German forces invaded the Soviet Union on 22 June 1941. This constituted 84 percent of the ADD force in the European portion of the Soviet Union. Most DB-3s and DB-3Fs were stationed away from border areas and escaped destruction from the initial Luftwaffe attacks.

The Ilyushins flew most early missions without fighter escort, due to communications failures among fighter and bomber unit commanders. This resulted in heavy DB-3 and DB-3F losses to Luftwaffe fighters. This prompted the Soviet Supreme Command to restrict DB-3s to night missions on 3 July 1941, although some daylight raids continued after this date. The four *Dal'nyi Aviatsionnyi Korpus* (DAK; Long-Range Aviation Corps) in the western Soviet Union had only 75 DB-3s and DB-3Fs available in late July of 1941. The high loss rate dropped considerably when the DB-3Fs began night missions. DB-3Fs/II-4s primarily carried 100-KG (220 pound) FAB-100 bombs, although 250-KG (551 pound) FAB-250 and 500-KG (1102 pound) FAB-500 bombs were also employed. Provisions were made to mount three VAP-500 or UChAP-500 chemical agent spray tanks under the fuselage, but these devices were never used in combat.

The VVS formed the ADD as an independent command subordinate to the *Stavka*[1] on 5 March 1942. The ADD consisted of eight DAKs with four DBAPs (Long-Range Bomber Aviation Regiments) per Corps. Each Regiment had three *Eskatrilyi* (Squadrons). Nominal strength of each DAK was 108 II-4s, with 27 aircraft per DBAP. II-4s were the bulk of ADD strength, but they were supplemented by B-25 Mitchells. Additional assets included Lisunov Li-2s (Soviet license-built Douglas DC-3s) and the US-supplied C-47 Skytrains (military DC-3s) converted into bombers.

II-4s flew several long-range attacks in August and September of 1942. These raids targeted Königsberg (now Kaliningrad, Russia), Danzig (now Gdansk, Poland), Berlin, Budapest in Hungary, and Bucharest in Romania. These missions lasted up to 12 hours and the pilot's work load was considerable with not every II-4 fitted with an autopilot. The navigator sometimes used his auxiliary controls in the nose to allow the pilot to relax. Such strategic missions were in the minority, as II-4s primarily flew tactical bombing mission that directly supported ground forces.

The II-4 added long-range reconnaissance, anti-aircraft suppression, and target marking to their bomber role during the conflict. The VVS put its long-range bombers back under its direct control when they transformed the ADD into the 18th VA on 8 December 1944. II-4s were among the 516 18th VA bombers that attacked Königsberg on 7 April 1945. This daylight raid supported an assault by the 3rd Belorussian Front.[2] This Air Army later deployed 743 bombers in attacking German defenses on the Oder River in eastern Germany.

Soviet DBAPs flew over 220,000 sorties and dropped over two million tons of bombs during the Great Patriotic War. Only 13,000 of these sorties were for strategic missions; the remainder were tactical in nature. During the Great Patriotic War, the Soviet Air Force lost over 10,000 bombers – including DB-3s and II-4s – in combat.

[1]*Stavka*: *Shtab Glavno/Verkovnovo Komandovaniya*; Chief of the Supreme Command Staff. This is the Russian term for their wartime armed forces high command.

[2]A Front is the Soviet/Russian equivalent of an Army Group (comprised of two or more Armies) in Western armies.

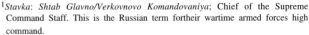

Mechanics prepare an II-4 (White 69) for a bombing mission against Axis targets in eastern Europe. The bombs were transported in wooden containers to the aircraft. This particular II-4 has the short exhaust stacks, which were lengthened to accommodate the GAM-9 flame damper on later production aircraft. The aircraft's upper surfaces appear to be Dark Green and Medium Green, while the undersurfaces are Black. This II-4 crew painted Otvazhnyi (Courageous) in White on the aft fuselage and over the Red star national insignia. (Viktor Kulikov)

Ground crews prepare a 500-ᴋɢ (1102 pound) FAB-500 bomb near an Il-4 (White 21) early in the Great Patriotic War. Tree branches rested against the airframe helped camouflage the bomber from German aircraft. The Il-4's Light Blue undersurfaces reflected brightly when caught by enemy searchlights during night missions. Most Il-4s built during the war were delivered with Black undersurfaces. (RART)

Il-4 Ordnance

100-ᴋɢ (220 pound) FAB-100 Bomb

250-ᴋɢ (551 pound) FAB-250 Bomb

500-ᴋɢ (1102 pound) FAB-500 Bomb

1000-ᴋɢ (2205 pound) FAB-1000 Bomb

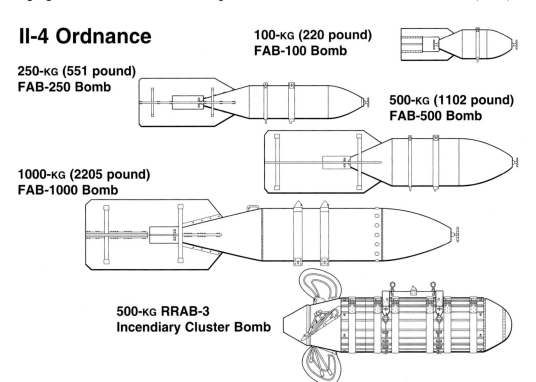

500-ᴋɢ RRAB-3 Incendiary Cluster Bomb

Ten 100-ᴋɢ (220 pound) FAB-100 bombs are lined up prior to loading into an Il-4. This aircraft carried a 1000-ᴋɢ (2205 pound) internal bomb load. An access ladder is propped up to the navigator-bombardier compartment opening. This Il-4 is equipped with long exhaust stacks capable of accommodating GAM-9 flame damping shrouds. (Viktor Kulikov)

German Ilyushin DB-3F

The Wehrmacht had launched Operation BARBAROSSA– the German invasion of the Soviet Union – on 22 June 1941. DB-3Fs assigned to the four Long-Range Bomber Aviation Corps in the Western Soviet Union were all based on airfields well to the rear. The Luftwaffe did not attack these airfields early in BARBAROSSA.

German troops captured several unserviceable DB-3Fs on their airfields as the Wehrmacht penetrated deeper into the Soviet Union. The Soviets destroyed unflyable Ilyushins whenever possible, but this was not always successful and several intact DB-3Fs were left for the Germans.

The Luftwaffe had knowledge of this aircraft before the conflict began, thanks to a DB-3M captured by Finnish forces during the 1939-40 Winter War. The *Ilmavoimat* (Finnish Air Force) loaned this aircraft (VP-13) to the Luftwaffe's Test and Evaluation Center at Rechlin. The DB-3M was flown to Germany on 12 May 1941 and tests were conducted at Rechlin until mid-September of 1941.

Components of captured DB-3Fs were also taken to the *Deutsche Versuchsanstalt fur Luftfahrt* (DVL; German Research Institute for Aviation) at Berlin-Adlershof for close examination. This process continued during the war, when new components not yet known to the Luftwaffe were found on captured or shot down Ilyushins.

The captured DB-3Fs were only used for test flights, due to their many technical shortcomings and poor flying characteristics. These bombers never saw action with the Luftwaffe's secret unit *Kampfgeschwader* (KG; Bomber Wing) 200, which flew captured Boeing B-17 Flying Fortress and Consolidated B-24 Liberator bombers.

German forces captured this DB-3F in the western Soviet Union in 1941. This bomber is painted Black and Olive Green on the upper surfaces and Light Blue on the undersurfaces. The Soviet red star was faintly overpainted on the vertical tail. German *Balkenkreuz* (Beam Cross) markings are painted on the rear fuselage, but the swastika is not placed on the tail. (Klaus Niska)

(Left) A Luftwaffe crew later painted a Yellow aft fuselage band to the same DB-3F. It is unusual that no German national markings were painted on the wing upper surfaces. The Luftwaffe tested captured DB-3Fs at its Test and Evaluation Center at Rechlin, Germany. Intact aircraft and components were evaluated to determine their strengths and weaknesses. Results from these tests enabled the Luftwaffe to determine the best tactics for engaging DB-3Fs/Il-4s. (Klaus Niska)

Finnish Ilyushin Il-4

The *Ilmavoimat* (Finnish Air Force) purchased four DB-3Fs (Il-4s) from German war booty stocks on 2 October 1942. The Ilyushins were handled over to the Finns at Bryansk on the Desna River, Soviet Union on 13 October 1942. These aircraft had a temporary overall RLM 04 Yellow (FS33538) finish over their Soviet camouflage for the ferry flight to Finland. All four DB-3Fs had German markings, which varied in size among the aircraft, and unoutlined tail swastikas. Finnish registrations DF-22 to DF-25 were painted as a kind of *Stammkennzeichen* (Root Markings). The *Stammkennzeichen* – usually a four-letter code – were always applied on German aircraft during ferry flights, when the aircraft had not been allocated to a combat unit.

One of these DB-3Fs (DF-22) crashed on approach to Syeshtshinskaya airfield on 14 October 1942. One of the M-88 engines failed prior to the aircraft landing at the field. The three remaining Il-4s (DF-23 through 25) safely reached Finland on 21 October.

Aircraft DF-24 and DF-25 were early DB-3Fs with the early conical engine cowling. The lower carburetor air intakes were stretched before the bombers were handed over to the Finns. Soviet Il-4s equipped with the early conical engine cowling normally had shorter carburetor air intakes. DF-24 lacked main landing gear doors for its ferry flight, but they were added after the bomber was overhauled in Finland.

The remaining Finnish Il-4 (DF-23) had the larger, less conical engine cowlings typical for later production Il-4s. This aircraft lacked the RPK-2 direction finding radio fitted to DF-24 and DF-25 and did not have its drop-shaped fairing on the port lower fuselage.

All three Il-4s were given a general overhaul after their arrival in Finland. They were painted Black and Medium Green on the upper surfaces and Light Blue on the undersurfaces. An RLM 04 Yellow aft fuselage band and lower wingtips identified an Axis aircraft on the Russian Front. DF-25 was retrofitted with larger exhaust stacks during its operational service.

The *Ilmavoimat* assigned the first overhauled Il-4 (DF-23) to the 2nd Flight of *Lentolaivue* (LeLv: Flying Squadron) 48 on 5 June 1943. This was followed by DF-25 on 30 July and DF-24 on 22 September. The first Finnish Il-4 combat mission occurred on the evening of 20 August 1943, when one aircraft attacked a partisan base west of Belomorsk. On 15 November 1943, the Il-4s of LeLv 48's 2nd Flight were reassigned to the new 3rd Flight of LeLv 46.

Carburetor Air Intake Development

Soviet Il-4

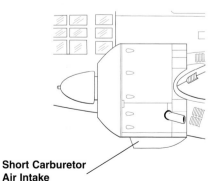

Short Carburetor Air Intake

Finnish Il-4

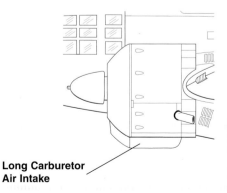

Long Carburetor Air Intake

The three Il-4s flew bombing missions against Soviet targets throughout late 1943 and well into 1944. DF-25's tail wheel broke away during a hard landing at Mensuvaara on 24 May 1944. This bomber was out of service for several weeks until it was repaired.

The RKKA (Red Army) began a major offensive in the Karelian Isthmus[1] on 9 June 1944. Finland's Il-4s were busy attacking Soviet positions that summer. One Il-4 (DF-24) was lost when it stalled on landing at Mensuvaara on 17 June 1944. The aircraft was initially considered salvageable and taken to a depot; however, the bomber was never repaired. The 3rd Flight of LeLv 46 flew its last combat mission against the Red Army on 8 August 1944, when a single Il-4 bombed the Suojärvi railroad station.

Finland sued for peace and signed an armistice with the Soviet Union on 4 September 1944. The Finns then turned on their former German allies in the Lapland War fought in northern Finland. Yellow fuselage bands and wingtips and national insignias – a light blue *Hakaristi* (swastika) on a white disc – were overpainted on Finnish Il-4s during this conflict. *Ilmavoimat* Il-4s flew their first missions against the Germans on 2 October 1944, when they bombed German troops in the Rovaniemi area. One Il-4 (DF-25) made a forced landing on a frozen lake and slid into shoreline woods on 3 January 1945. This bomber was damaged beyond economical repair. The Finnish Il-4s flew nine missions against retreating German forces during the Lapland War.

Only one Il-4 (DF-23) of the four received from the Germans in 1941 survived World War Two. This aircraft was flown to a storage depot on 23 February 1945, after logging 169 flying hours in *Ilmavoimat* service. Finland's national marking was changed to a white, light blue, and white roundel on 1 April 1945. These new markings were painted on DF-23 in the storage depot, although it never flew again.

[1]The Karelian Isthmus separating southeastern Finland from northwestern Russia was fought over in the 1939-40 Winter War.

German crews prepare a captured Il-4 (DF-23) for its ferry flight from Bryansk, Soviet Union to Finland. The upper surface camouflage was overpainted Yellow and German markings were applied. It has new conical engine cowlings, but not the standard RPK-2 direction finder on the lower nose. DF-23 was the only Finnish Il-4 to survive World War Two. (Klaus Niska)

Another Il-4 (DF-24) touches down on Finnish soil after the ferry flight from Bryansk. This particular Ilyushin was missing its main landing gear doors. The lower wing *Balkenkreuz* has a thin White outline. DF-24 was the first Finnish Il-4 lost, when it crash-landed at Mensuvaara on 17 June 1944. (Klaus Niska)

An Il-4 (DF-25) is readied for a mission during the Lapland War in mid-1944, in which the Germans were driven out of Finland. *Ilmavoimat* (Finnish Air Force) DB-3Ms and Il-4s had their yellow identification markings and national insignias overpainted for this conflict. DF-25 was damaged beyond repair by a forced landing on a frozen lake on 3 January 1945. (Klaus Niska)

The tail wheel of this Il-4 (DF-25) collapsed during a hard landing at Mensuvaara airbase on 24 May 1944. At that time, the Ilyushin was assigned to the 3rd Flight of LeLv (Flying Squadron) 46. Nearly a third of the outer wing undersurfaces were painted RLM04 Yellow to identify Axis aircraft on the Russian Front. (Klaus Niska)

The starboard M-88 engine is test run on this Finnish Il-4 (DF-25). Finnish technicians lengthened the exhaust stacks and the carburetor air intakes during overhauls after delivery from German-occupied Soviet territory. Soviet Il-4s equipped with the early conical engine cowling had a shorter carburetor air intake. (Klaus Niska)

Ilyushin Il-4T

Ilyushin developed a torpedo carrying aircraft for the VVS VMF (Soviet Naval Aviation) in parallel to the Il-4 bomber. This variant was designated the **Il-4T** (*torpedonosyets*; torpedo carrier) and was modified through its production cycle in a similar way to the Il-4 bomber.

Many Il-4Ts were fitted with an RPK-2 Radio Direction Finder (RDF) antenna in a teardrop-shaped fairing atop the nose in front of the windshield. Il-4 bombers had the RPK-2 mounted on the lower port nose section. Some Il-4Ts replaced the RPK-2 with an RPK-10 direction finding radio, which had a loop antenna. A second venturi tube was mounted under the port cockpit sill on some Il-4Ts, and other aircraft had protective material placed over the glazed nose hatch.

Several Il-4Ts had a large window fitted to both sides of the nose. This improved the exterior view for the navigator, who launched the torpedo.

One 45-CM (17.7 inch) torpedo was mounted on a T-18 centerline pylon under the fuselage. The VMF employed the Type 45-36-AN torpedo for low altitude release and the Type 45-36-AM for shallow waters. The Type 45-36-AV was dropped from an altitude between 250 M (820 feet) and 400 M (1312 feet). The torpedo could be replaced by an externally mounted sea mine, either the 900-KG (1984 pound) AMG-1 or the 1000-KG (2205 pound) *Geyro* anchored mine. External racks mounted on the lower fuselage held two 500-KG (1102 pound) MDM-500 seabed mines.

The Il-4T's first combat mission occurred on 25 June 1941, three days after German forces invaded the Soviet Union. Aircraft of the 2nd *Mino-Torpednaya Aviatsiya Polk* (MTAP; Mine-Torpedo Aviation Regiment), VVS of the *Chernomorskii Flot* (ChF; Black Sea Fleet) attacked Constanta harbor, Romania. The raid employed conventional bombs and caused light damage.

Seven Il-4Ts from this Regiment bombed the Romanian capital of Bucharest on 8 August 1941. VVS ChF Il-4Ts were active until August of 1944.

The 1st MTAP, VVS of the *Krasnoznamyonny Baltiiski Flot* (KBF; Red Banner Baltic Fleet) received its first Il-4Ts in August of 1941. They were primarily employed for conventional bombing of enemy positions until the spring of 1942. Il-4Ts also dropped mines outside the ports of Helsinki and Kotka in Finland and Tallinn, Estonia. Most of these missions were flown at night. The Regiment flew its first torpedo mission in mid-1942. Il-4Ts of the 1st MTAP sank 17 Axis vessels in 81 sorties in the summer of 1942. During 1943, the Regiment made 93 torpedo attacks that sank 43 German vessels.

The VVS of the *Severnyi Flot* (SF; Northern Fleet) received its first Il-4T in September of 1941. They initially bombed enemy airfields, but two Il-4Ts assigned to the 2nd Guards Composite Aviation Regiment destroyed an enemy vessel in the Porsanger-Fiord in northern Norway on 29 July 1942.

The final Il-4 combat operations occurred in the Far East, after the Soviet Union declared war on Japan on 8 August 1945 – two days after the first atomic bomb was dropped on Hiroshima, Japan. The RKKA (Red Army) invaded Manchuria and Korea, under occupation by the Japanese Kwantung Army. The 19th *Dalni Aviatsionnyi Korpus* (DAK; Long-Range Aviation Corps), VVS of the *Tikhookyeanskii Flot* (TOF; Pacific Fleet) flew 157 Il-4Ts for torpedo dropping and conventional bombing missions. The 4th MTAP's Il-4Ts bombed the port of Rasin, Korea on 9 August. The next night, 76 Il-4Ts bombed Changchung and Charbin in Manchuria. Japanese fighter opposition was so weak during this period that the Il-4Ts began flying daylight missions. During the 25 days of war with Japan, the 19th DAK's Il-4Ts sank 15 vessels by torpedo attacks.

The Il-4T continued to serve in VVS VMF Mine-Torpedo Aviation Regiments until 1952, when it was replaced by the jet-powered Ilyushin Il-28T (ASCC code name Beagle).

A 45-CM (17.7 inch) Type 45-36-AV torpedo is mounted on an Il-4T assigned to the VVS KBF (Red Banner Baltic Fleet Air Force). This weapon is launched from an altitude between 250 M (820 feet) and 400 M (1312 feet). The parachute container is mounted onto the torpedo's tail section. Protective materials cover the nose entry hatch. (RART)

VMF (Soviet Navy) crewmen load a black Type 45-36-AN torpedo onto an early Il-4T. This weapon was optimized for launching at 30 M (98 feet). A non-standard pitot tube is mounted on the port nose, while long exhaust stacks protrude from the engine cowlings. This Il-4's nose entry hatch is covered by protective material. (Viktor Kulikov)

Il-4T Nose Development

Il-4T (Standard)

RPK-2 Radio Direction Finding (RDF) Antenna

Small Windows on Port Side

Il-4T (Modified)

RPK-10 RDF Antenna

Large Window on Port Side

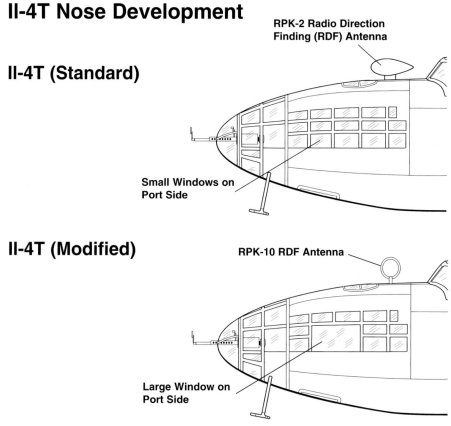

Natural metal Type 45-36-ANs are mounted on carts prior to loading on aircraft, including an Il-4T (Yellow 10). Each 940 KG (2072 pound) torpedo was mounted on a cart, which was manually moved. The Type 45-36 was a copy of the Italian *Fiume* (River) torpedo. Three ship silhouettes painted on the Il-4's tail represented Axis ships this torpedo aircraft sank. (RART)

A loop-shaped RPK-10 Radio Direction Finder (RDF) antenna is mounted on this Il-4T's upper nose, between the antenna mast and the windshield. A large window is mounted in the nose section's port side, while dust filters were placed over the carburetor air intakes.

45-CM (17.7-Inch) Torpedoes

Type 45-36-AN (Low Altitude)

Type 45-36-AV (High Altitude)

Brake Parachute Container

Type 45-36-AM (Shallow Water)

Metal Plate to Reduce Torpedo's Dive into the Water

An Il-4T (White 13) armed with a Type 45-36-AV torpedo taxies to the runway at the start of a mission. A cylindrical housing attached to the torpedo's tail housed a brake parachute, which opened on release from the aircraft. This parachute slowed the weapon's fall to the water and was jettisoned upon impact with the water. Most Il-4Ts retained their original Light Blue undersurfaces. (Viktor Kulikov)

A 900-KG (1984 pound) AMG-1 sea mine is loaded on the centerline pylon of this late production Il-4T. The 3.5 M (11.5 foot) long mine was dropped from the aircraft over coastal waters. Moveable shutters fitted to the engine cowlings helped regulate the flow of cooling air during extreme cold weather. GAM-9 flame dampers are mounted to the exhausts of this Il-4T, whose undersurface was painted Black. (Viktor Kulikov)

VMF armorers push an AMG-1 sea mine towards an awaiting Il-4T. This aircraft is equipped with an RPK-2 RDF in a teardrop-shaped fairing atop the nose. Il-4Ts normally had the RPK-2 mounted on the upper nose surface, instead of the lower nose as on Il-4 bombers. (Viktor Kulikov)

900-KG (1984-Pound) AMG-1 Sea Mine

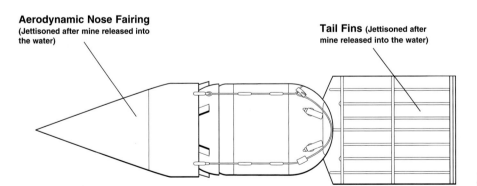

Aerodynamic Nose Fairing (Jettisoned after mine released into the water)

Tail Fins (Jettisoned after mine released into the water)

Ilyushin Il-4 Transport

Partisan warfare became an effective part of Soviet strategy from 1943. A total of 1.4 million partisans were active in the German-occupied territory of the western Soviet Union. They were organized in approximately 6200 different partisan formations. During the Great Patriotic War, these guerrilla formations had destroyed 10,000 locomotives, 110,000 railroad cars, 12,000 bridges, and 65,000 motor vehicles.

A partisan headquarters was established in Moscow in May of 1942 for directing units and attempting to organize radio contacts and parachute drops. It became important to provide the partisans operating deep inside enemy territory with the necessary equipment, including radios, weapons and ammunition, and items to sabotage enemy railroads and communications.

During the Great Patriotic War, most partisan supply missions were flown either by the Lisunov Li-2 – the Soviet license-built version of the Douglas DC-3 transport – or C-47s (military version of the DC-3) supplied by the US under Lend-Lease. The 10th Guards Aviation Transport Division flew over 340,000 partisans and agents behind German lines. Additionally, 52,000 tons of ammunition were supplied to the partisans and 44,000 wounded guerrilla fighters were evacuated to hospitals.

Il-4s were used to transport items that were too bulky for the Li-2 or the C-47. Platforms attached to the centerline pylon under the fuselage held bulky items, including anti-tank guns, motorcycles, and sidecars. Wooden aerodynamic fairings were placed on the anti-tank guns to reduce drag during flight. These covers were easily removed after landing and the weapon was ready for action after only a short preparation time.

The VVS developed the UDP-500 container to paradrop supplies to partisans and spies. This bomb-shaped container held up to 500 KG (1102 pounds) of weapons, ammunition, radios, and clothing. The Il-4 carried up to three UDP-500s on fuselage pylons.

Specially converted Il-4s were used on partisan supply missions between 1943 and 1944. Most of these missions were flown at night deep into enemy territory. Il-4s deployed on partisan missions were drawn from VVS Long-Range Aviation Regiments.

A motorcycle and sidecar are loaded under the fuselage of this ADD (Long-Range Aviation) Il-4. Motorcycles were airlifted to partisan units operating behind Axis lines and enhanced their mobility in mounting hit-and-run attacks. (Viktor Kulikov)

A 45MM anti-tank gun mounted on a platform is loaded under a late production Il-4. A wooden aerodynamic covering over the gun reduced drag during flight. The Il-4 was mainly used to airlift equipment too bulky for either the Lisunov Li-2 (license-built Douglas DC-3) or the Lend-Lease supplied C-47 (DC-3 military variant). (Viktor Kulikov)

A drag-reducing wooden fairing covered the anti-tank gun for its air delivery. This weapon is mounted on the Il-4's centerline pylon and dropped by parachute. The fairing was removed after the gun landed on the ground. (RART)

Ilyushin Il-4TK

Il-4s suffered heavy losses when they flew their first daylight missions in the Great Patriotic War. One of the aircraft's handicaps was its insufficient ceiling with a full bomb load. The VVS needed a bomber that could operate above the ceiling of German fighters.

The Ilyushin OKB (Experimental Design Bureau) developed the **Il-4TK** (*turbo kompressor*) high altitude bomber in 1942. This Il-4 variant featured a pressurized cabin for the pilot and the navigator. The high altitude Il-4TK was designed for either bombing or reconnaissance missions. It was intended to operate at 11,000 м (36,089 feet), which was well above the range of German anti-aircraft guns and was at least level with Luftwaffe fighters.

Two different nose sections were evaluated before the Il-4TK prototype was built. One version had a remotely controlled machine gun barbette. Problems encountered in developing this weapon ended consideration of this nose section. Ilyushin then chose a hemispheric nose without armament. The Il-4TK lacked defensive armament and relied on its high altitude capabilities for its best defense against enemy fighters. Both the MV-3 dorsal turret and the MV-2 nose turret on standard production Il-4s were deleted. The pitot head was moved from the lower side of the Il-4's nose to atop the Il-4TK's nose.

The pilot was seated in front of the navigator in the ventilation type pressurized cabin. No radio operator or rear gunner was carried aboard the Il-4TK. Cabin pressurization differential was adjusted through a system of valves, while the cabin temperature was maintained using an air radiator. Air was fed from the TK-3 turbo-superchargers and filtered before going to the pressurized cabin.

A pitot tube was added to the Il-4TK's port wing leading edge, while large carburetor air intakes on the lower engine cowlings were deleted. A remotely controlled AFA-3 camera was mounted in the tail section. The additional equipment brought the Il-4TK's take off weight to 10,593 кг (23,353 pounds), which was approximately 400 кг (882 pounds) heavier than for the standard Il-4.

TK-3 turbo superchargers developed by the TsIAM (Central Institute of Aircraft Engines) boosted power to both M-88B engines. The TK-3 was first used on the M-25 engine that powered the Polikarpov I-153V high-altitude fighter in 1939. This turbo supercharger enabled the M-88B to sustain between 875 HP and 880 HP at high altitude. The TK-3s were mounted on the aft engine nacelle undersurfaces. This location was well away from the fuel tanks and reduced the potential fire hazard if there was a malfunction in the exhaust gas-driven turbo supercharger.

The pilot started the TK-3 by closing their shutters, which directed engine exhaust gases to the turbo supercharger. These gases spun the TK-3's compressor blades up to 23,000 RPM. Compressed air from the turbo supercharger was then fed to the M-88B's carburetor.

Major-General Vladimir K. Kokkinaki – then the chief inspector of the Soviet aviation industry – was at the controls for the Il-4TK's initial flight on 16 March 1943. This and subsequent test flights revealed that the TK-3s could not deliver the planned power increase while the VISh-61-IF propellers failed to produce the required thrust. The aircraft reached a maximum ceiling of 9300 м (30,512 feet) during factory trials, which was approximately 1700 м (5577 feet) short of the specification. Additionally, the M-88B and TK-3 combination proved troublesome and too delicate for operation by regular ADD (Long-Range Aviation) units in the harsh frontline environment.

The Ilyushin OKB considered installing more advanced TK-M turbo superchargers and substituting AV-9F high-altitude propellers for the VISh-61-IFs. These planned improvements were not implemented and the Il-4TK program was cancelled. A strong German Luftwaffe justified Soviet research for a high-altitude bomber in 1942; however, this situation had changed from the fall of 1943, when the VVS held air superiority over the Eastern Front. The Soviets no longer felt a need for a high-altitude bomber when its tasks were performed by the standard Il-4.

The Il-4TK had been developed as a high-altitude bomber able to fly higher than German anti-aircraft fire and fighters. The entire nose section was redesigned with a fully glazed front section. The two-man crew – pilot and navigator-bombardier – was located in the pressurized capsule. TK-3 superchargers boosted the power of the two M-88B engines, which enabled the aircraft to reach 9300 м (30,512 feet). The Il-4TK did not carry any armament. (Viktor Kulikov)

Ilyushin Il-6

The Ilyushin OKB began studying a successor to the Il-4 in mid-1942. This new bomber was intended to have similar overall performance to the Il-4, but with a 100 кмн (62 мрн) higher cruising speed than the earlier aircraft. Ilyushin learned from the combat experience of Il-4 crews and one objective of this new design was to eliminate most of the Il-4's shortcomings. It became necessary to improve both the defensive armament and the crew's armor protection. This new bomber would have two pilots, instead of the Il-4's single pilot.

Intended powerplant for this new bomber was a pair of 2000 нр ASh-71 (M-71) 18-cylinder, air-cooled, radial engines. Arcadiy D. Shvetsov developed this engine in 1941 by combining two M-63 nine-cylinder radial engines into a two-row powerplant with direct fuel injection.

This concept impressed the VVS (Soviet Air Force), which ordered one prototype designated **Il-6**. The VVS decided early in development to replace the gasoline-powered ASh-71s by two 1500 нр ACh-30B 12-cylinder, liquid-cooled, inline diesel engines. A.D. Charomsky developed this powerplant, which weighed 1150 кg (2535 pounds). A turbo supercharger enabled the ACh-30B to maintain 1200 нр at 6000 м (19,685 feet). This diesel engine consumed 40 percent less fuel than the ASh-71 aviation gasoline powerplant. Diesel fuel was less expensive, easier to produce, and was in greater supply than 92-octane aviation gasoline.

Diesel engines had a drawback in their heavier overall weight compared to comparable gasoline powerplants. Soviet engineers calculated that missions exceeding five hours were more economically performed with diesel fuel than with gasoline. The same calculation showed that a diesel-powered bomber could carry twice the bomb load from Moscow to Berlin than a conventional bomber.

The Il-6 prototype was completed at GAZ (State Aviation Factory) 39 at Irkutsk and first flew on 7 August 1943. Oil coolers are flush mounted in the wing leading edges, which are swept back at a greater angle than on the Il-4. This aircraft was painted with Medium Green upper surfaces and Flat Black undersurfaces. Several Il-2 Shturmovik attack aircraft are parked behind the Il-6 prototype. (Viktor Kulikov)

The Il-6 featured a newly designed wing incorporating a large leading edge sweep angle and straight trailing edge. Each ASh-71 was installed in a streamlined nacelle, with an oil cooler fitted below the cowling. Radiator inlets flanked both nacelle sides on the leading edge, with the radiators mounted inside the wing inboard section. Exhaust flaps were located on the lower wing surface and were adjusted by the pilot.

The rear reinforcing strip fitted to the Il-4 fuselage was deleted on the Il-6, which had an oval window installed on each rear fuselage side. Main landing gear doors fitted flush to the nacelles and lacked the two blisters per door found on the Il-4. A square window was placed on each side of the dorsal fairing, while the long entry handhold rail on the port fuselage side was deleted. The Il-6 had an angled upper rudder without mass balance weights, while the Il-4 had a straight rudder with a balance weight mounted atop the rudder.

The Il-6 had a wingspan of 26.07 м (85 feet 6.4 inches), which was 4.63 м (15 feet 2.3 inches) longer than the Il-4's 21.44 м (70 feet 4.1 inch) span. The new bomber's length of 17.38 м (57 feet) was 2.6 м (8 feet 6 inches) longer than the Il-4's 14.79 м (48 feet 6.3 inch) length. This aircraft's height is unknown. Empty weight of the Il-6 was 11,690 кg (25,772 pounds), while its maximum take off weight was 18,650 кg (41,116 pounds).

A crew of six manned the Il-6, including the navigator in the glazed nose, pilot and co-pilot side-by-side on the flight deck, a radio operator, and two gunners. All crew stations were protected by a total of 400 кg (882 pounds) of armor.

Defensive armament consisted of five 20мм Shiptal'nyi/Vladimirov ShVAK cannon in single mounts. One weapon was mounted in the nose, two in waist positions in the fuselage, a fourth gun in a dorsal turret, and the fifth cannon in an aft-facing ventral fairing. The Il-6's maximum bomb load was 2000 кg (4409 pounds), with up to four 500-кg (1102 pound) bombs carried internally. Additionally, two fuselage undersurface hardpoints held either two 1000-кg (2205 pound) bombs or two torpedoes.

The Il-6 was built in the experimental shop of GAZ (State Aviation Factory) 39 at Irkutsk and was ready for trials in the summer of 1943. Major-General Vladimir K. Kokkinaki conducted the initial flight on 7 August 1943. Trials demonstrated the ACh-30Bs provided insufficient power for the aircraft. Engineers lightened the Il-6 by removing armament and armor plating, while the crew was limited to five men. The aircraft was painted with Medium Green upper surfaces and Flat Black undersurfaces.

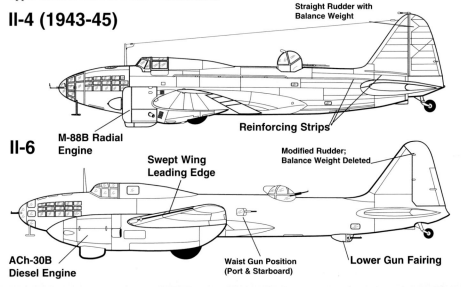

Il-4 (1943-45)

Straight Rudder with Balance Weight

M-88B Radial Engine

Reinforcing Strips

Il-6

Swept Wing Leading Edge

Modified Rudder; Balance Weight Deleted

ACh-30B Diesel Engine

Waist Gun Position (Port & Starboard)

Lower Gun Fairing

The eight-month long factory trials were exceptionally lengthy and revealed a number of shortcomings. Most of these problems were related with the unreliable ACh-30B diesel engines. Another shortcoming was the Il-6's extremely poor controllability, particularly on the landing approach. The Il-6 was assigned to the *Letno-Issledovatel'skii Institut* (LII; Flight Research Institute) at Kratovo (now Zhukovsky) between April and May of 1944 to overcome these problems. The LII recommended moving the center of gravity aft in order to aid the aircraft's controllability. They also suggested that Ilyushin change the elevators' shape and decrease its area.

Ilyushin reequipped the Il-6 with ACh-30BF diesel engines in the summer of 1944. This powerplant's output was 1900 HP at take off and 1500 HP at 6000 M (19,685 feet). The ACh-30BF's reliability was enhanced over the ACh-30B by a double-stage injection system, which used aviation gasoline in the first stage and kerosene injected into the carburetor in the second stage. Installation of the more powerful ACh-30BFs allowed the fitting of the intended armament and armor plating.

The revised Il-6 prototype reached a maximum speed of 464 KMH (288 MPH) during factory trials held in the summer of 1944. Ilyushin's new bomber had a range of 5450 KM (3387 miles) with a 1000 KG (2205 pound) bomb load and a cruising speed of 340 KMH (211 MPH). The service ceiling was 6200 M (20,341 feet). These trials also revealed the high wing load, which required higher speeds for approach and landing. In turn, this required longer runways that were not always available at the front.

This aircraft was reassigned to the LII after the factory test trials. Tests at Kratovo revealed difficulties in starting the ACh-30BF engine, which took a long time to reach its maximum revolutions per minute (RPM). This made the engine too difficult to operate under frontline conditions. It became clear that an Il-6 engine reequipment program would likely take longer than the war with Germany, resulting in cancellation of this new bomber. The sole Il-6 built was the last piston engine bomber developed by the Ilyushin OKB, which began developing jet powered bombers soon after the Great Patriotic War ended on 9 May 1945.

(Above) The Il-6 rests between test flights during its trials in the summer of 1944. ACh-30BF inline diesel engines replaced the ASh-71 inline gasoline engines originally fitted to the aircraft. The Il-6 was armed with five 20MM ShVAK cannon, including single guns in port and starboard waist positions and in the lower aft fuselage fairing. White-bordered Red stars are painted on the vertical tail and aft fuselage, but not on the wing upper surfaces. (Viktor Kulikov)

(Below) The Il-6's modified upper rudder provided mass balance. This replaced the mass balance weight used atop the Il-4's rudder. The Il-6 was the last piston engine bomber developed by the Ilyushin OKB (Experimental Design Bureau). Further development of the sole Il-6 built was terminated in the fall of 1944. (Viktor Kulikov)

More Men and Machines from
squadron/signal publications

Aircraft in Action

1043 P-39 Airacobra

Armor in Action

2020 T-34

Walk Around

5516 B-17 Flying Fortress

Combat Troops in Action

2 German Infantry

Detail & Scale

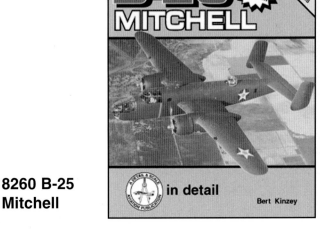

8260 B-25 Mitchell

Warships in Action

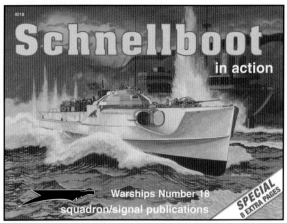

4018 Schnellboot